NKUMBA
An African Challenge

Today much of Africa is troubled. Perhaps in 1971 Zambia was less so, but it still had poverty, shanty towns, border closures and banditry. The ebb and flow of world copper prices was reflected in the prosperity or otherwise of the country and the wellbeing of its people. The sun is ever-present in Zambia, with sunsets that are breathtaking swathes of colour. Sometimes the throb of drums will carry on the night air, telling of some celebration deep in the bush. The drums seem to speak of an ancient culture unchanged by the passing years — but there is much going on beneath the surface; there is much to tell.

Books by Ian Campbell Thomson
Published by The House of Ulverscroft:

THE HIRED LAD
MOGFORD'S WINNING WAYS
MANAGER BY APPOINTMENT

IAN CAMPBELL THOMSON

NKUMBA
An African Challenge

Complete and Unabridged

ULVERSCROFT
Leicester

First published in Great Britain in 2010 by
Drum Publishing
Oxford

First Large Print Edition
published 2014
by arrangement with
Drum Publishing
Oxford

A catalogue record for this book is available
from the British Library.

ISBN 978–1–4448–2076–8

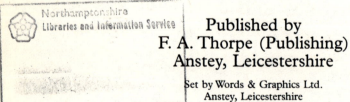

Published by
F. A. Thorpe (Publishing)
Anstey, Leicestershire

Set by Words & Graphics Ltd.
Anstey, Leicestershire
Printed and bound in Great Britain by
T. J. International Ltd., Padstow, Cornwall

This book is printed on acid-free paper

Acknowledgements

With thanks for help and encouragement:

Clare Hartzler
Greta Withers

SPECIAL ⌒ *80003488886* ERS

THE ULVERSCROFT FOUNDATION
(registered UK charity number 264873)
was established in 1972 to provide funds for
research, diagnosis and treatment of eye diseases.
Examples of major projects funded by
the Ulverscroft Foundation are:-

- The Children's Eye Unit at Moorfields Eye Hospital, London
- The Ulverscroft Children's Eye Unit at Great Ormond Street Hospital for Sick Children
- Funding research into eye diseases and treatment at the Department of Ophthalmology, University of Leicester
- The Ulverscroft Vision Research Group, Institute of Child Health
- Twin operating theatres at the Western Ophthalmic Hospital, London
- The Chair of Ophthalmology at the Royal Australian College of Ophthalmologists

You can help further the work of the Foundation
by making a donation or leaving a legacy.
Every contribution is gratefully received. If you
would like to help support the Foundation or
require further information, please contact:

THE ULVERSCROFT FOUNDATION
The Green, Bradgate Road, Anstey
Leicester LE7 7FU, England
Tel: (0116) 236 4325

website: www.foundation.ulverscroft.com

1

Decision Time

A life-changing happening can come along in many guises. Sometimes it is the result of deliberate application in some direction but more often than not it is chance. In my case my move from Devon to Africa in 1970 started as a light hearted job application with what seemed very little chance of success.

We had been persuaded to sell our thirty six acres of steep land — which we had been farming part-time for eight years — by a persistent bidder who had come up with a final offer we would have been foolish to refuse. Having cleared our obligation to the bank we were able to buy a plot of land in the nearby village and have a house built on it. I continued to work on a large pig farm where I had been employed for the last six years. My wife Renee was employed in the offices of a national bakery.

Although I had considerable responsibility for the day to day running of the pig unit I missed being in overall charge. Indeed I had reached a stage where I needed to get back into management. Local opportunities in this direction were non-existent and with a son and daughter happily entrenched at Barnstaple Grammar School I was unwilling to drag the family off to some other part of the country where management positions might have been on offer.

It was with this background that it all started. My wife Renee spotted an advertisement in a newspaper.

'This would suit you,' she said cheerfully, little knowing where it was to lead.

In essence the advertisement stated that The Rural Development Corporation of Zambia was in urgent need of someone to manage a 500-sow pig unit together with some arable farming. The conditions were set out: salary, terminal bonus after three years, free flights, six weeks annual leave, boarding school fees.

'Not a hope,' I said.

'Worth a try. You've always wanted to see Africa. All that big game, sunsets, getting away from the Devon rainfall.'

We joked about it but eventually decided, yes, it was worth a try, a bit of fun, nothing to lose, we sent a letter.

I was sure I had the right background for the job but suspected it would attract a large number of more highly qualified people. The

2

letter posted, we thought no more about it and got on with our lives.

Three months passed and, much to my surprise, I had a letter asking me to attend the Zambian High Commission in London for an interview. I would be interviewed by Mr Kapota who was the General Manager of The Rural Development Corporation of Zambia. Well, there was nothing to lose by attending an expenses-paid interview.

Mr Kapota turned out to be a friendly, affable man of considerable stature and presence. He greeted me warmly and pointed out that they needed expertise to produce pigs for domestic consumption, grow maize likewise and train a Zambian to take over at the end of the three-year contract on offer. He explained everything fully: 4,170 acres of land, probably about 800 acres in cultivation. Maize would be the crop but they had sunflowers also in mind. He questioned me in some detail about my experience and finally required some input from me. I went over the details of the conditions of employment to be quite sure I understood everything correctly. Mr Kapota agreed that I had, but said, 'the successful applicant will be sent a contract with every detail covered.' I made sure there was an abattoir and feed mill facilities and asked about housing for the pigs.

'This will be done before a Manager is appointed. If you are successful you will be notified.' As we shook hands he said, 'In the morning I am off to Denmark to interview another applicant.'

I travelled home thinking that it had been an interesting experience but I was far from confident. Mr Kapota was obviously prepared to travel the world to get the right person. Indeed I heard nothing for the best part of a year, then one evening the telephone rang. 'We have decided to offer you the job,' a voice said. 'You will get a letter in the post if you agree, giving all details. I hope you will accept now and I can send you a contract. When you return this I will send your travel documents.'

My head was spinning. 'But when would you expect me to start?' I managed.

'As soon as possible. If you say now you want the job I will get a contract to you for signature.'

'Am I talking to Mr Kapota?'

'No Sir. I work for him in London at the High Commission. Do you want the job?'

'Yes,' I said weakly. 'Thank you.' I replaced the phone.

From this point on there was much heart searching. The children were happy at school. Boarding school didn't appeal. Finally it was decided I should go alone and test the water.

Reasonable commutes might keep Renee and me happy and the children could come out for school holidays.

A flurry of activity followed. Some shopping for a warm climate; lightweight shirts and slacks seemed a safe bet. A visit to our doctor who advised on and dealt with my various obligatory injections. One he could not supply was yellow fever; I would have to make arrangements with a doctor at the nearby R.A.F. base. I duly made an appointment and reported on time. I was informed that my doctor was playing hockey. I found the hockey field and stood on the touchline. Either someone had alerted the good doctor or he put two and two together as during a lull he dashed over. 'Only another ten minutes, bear with me.' I said I would and was duly injected by a sweaty doctor still in his strip. I had a slight fever as a result but was fine when I woke in the morning.

And so it was, with my mind in a whirl and my emotions pulling me this way and that, I found myself on a December day in 1970 boarding a train for Exeter; another train to Reading; the rail link bus to Heathrow to board a night flight to Zambia. At forty-seven years of age I had never flown or even been in an airport.

It might seem strange in this age of

frequent air travel that it was not always thus. This naivety was soon spotted by my travelling companions. Two little girls occupied the inner seats. They would have been perhaps eleven and eight respectively and obviously seasoned travellers. Perhaps it was my initial fumble with my seat belt which alerted the girls and with the directness that goes with being a child, the younger one asked, 'Is this your first flight?' When I confessed that it was they insisted that I have the window seat so that I could witness the take-off. Generally taking me in hand the elder one said, 'there may be air pockets as we take off over Heathrow. The plane drops a bit; you get a funny feeling in your tum. We will get a meal on the way to Rome. We stop to re-fuel or something; then down over Italy and the Sahara desert. I expect we will be asleep by then.' I was grateful for their chatter. Their dad worked in the Copperbelt. They were going out for the Christmas holiday; they had done this trip several times. Yes they missed their mum and dad but boarding school was OK. I had no idea, as children travelling alone, whether they were being supervised by the cabin staff, but I suppose they may have been. They hardly needed it, they were well seasoned travellers.

Flying over the Alps in the moonlight for

the first time was memorable. Sharp peaks and deep valleys with twinkling lights far below. Why I should have been surprised to see the toe of Italy looking just as it does on a map I don't know, it was all thrilling and then the Sahara. The lights were dimmed, we were issued with blankets and soon sleep took over. I awoke to blue skies, clouds like puffs of cotton wool and brilliant sunshine. Eventually the sand dunes gave way to scrub bush, small settlements could be spotted. We had left the seemingly endless desert behind and were moving toward a more recognisable Africa.

Captain Brown brought the DC8 down to a smooth landing. I was always comforted by his presence up front on future flights. His brisk, alert bearing was reassuring and the greying hair indicated years of experience. Zambia Airways at one time had a less than perfect safety record but, now managed by Alitalia, recent history had been good.

We disembarked in brilliant sunshine and set off on foot for the airport buildings; my two young friends skipping along on either side of me, chatting across me and obviously excited by the prospect of being re-united with their parents and home not much more than an hour away in Ndola.

Inside the airport building they made sure I

knew how to collect my luggage and where to queue for passport inspection, then they dashed off to join the people lining up for an internal flight. I watched them scamper across the concourse; as they neared their queue they turned and walking backwards waved their goodbyes. I waved back marvelling at their self-assurance.

Formalities over, I hefted my suitcase and walked across the foyer; all very smart with a fountain playing at its centre. A woman walked past, she had a packet of cigarettes on her head. Her walk was graceful, her balance perfect. I realised that the brightly coloured wrap-around skirt which she wore would have no pockets. I was also aware of all the bright colours being worn all around me and the sunlight shafting in everywhere. The London I had left had been drab and grey with people on the streets muffled against the cold. By the exit a large uniformed black man sat. I supposed he was a security man or a policeman. I waited; after a few minutes the uniformed gentleman caught my eye.

'You waiting Bwana. Someone to come?'

I explained that I was expecting to be met by someone from the Rural Development Corporation.

'Is OK.,' he said. 'He come soon.'

I had already experienced two firsts. I had

been called Bwana and I had encountered what, I was to learn later, expatriates referred to as the Z factor; a rather casual, relaxed approach by Zambians to time.

Twenty minutes passed then a car drew up and a small man alighted. He shook my hand effusively, made no excuses for his lateness and insisted on carrying my suitcase.

We sped down a rather fine highway to join the melee of traffic on the Great East Road and so into Lusaka. Parked opposite the Lusaka Hotel my escort took my hand to conduct me through the bustle of horn blowing traffic. I was not too keen on this hand holding, but it was, I discovered, a friendly gesture not uncommon in Africa.

My situation was explained at the desk. I was booked in and then I was whisked off to meet my employers at the company headquarters, a prestigious building called Kwacha House. In a top floor office I renewed my acquaintance with Mr Kapota who came from behind his desk to shake hands and bid me welcome. He then turned to introduce another smartly-suited gentleman. 'Mr Banda,' he explained, 'is our link with the government; used to be our High Commissioner in U.S.A.; I think he had a good time over there.'

Mr Banda shook hands. 'We are glad to

welcome you, we need your expertise.' He smiled broadly. 'Mr Kapota is right, I enjoyed my time in America. I was in New York when the power failed. People stuck in lifts all over the place; the city came to a standstill. Now, coffee.' He indicated a coffee table and comfortable chairs. We seated ourselves and coffee appeared from somewhere.

'Now,' said Mr Kapota with a show of briskness, 'you must have questions?'

'Not really,' I said. 'We covered everything very thoroughly at my interview. The Corporation is quasi-government; funded initially by the government but expected to be self-supporting in due course. You require me to supply 8,000 pork and bacon carcasses per annum for domestic consumption and also I have some arable farming to do. I would though, like to know when I might start.'

The two men exchanged glances. The smiles became rather fixed. Mr Kapota cleared his throat. 'I'm afraid your house is not quite ready, it is being painted and you will need furniture.'

'But if I have transport I can get out there and have a look around.' There was an awkward pause, then Mr Kapota offered. 'I'm afraid your vehicle is not quite available yet. You will have a Toyota vanette as soon as possible. However I will arrange for Skottke to call at your hotel and sort everything out. Skottke is overall projects manager; tobacco development, dairy development, beef cattle; you are farm development. Your farm is called Nkumba. Skottke will see to all the details.' The smiles were back in place. 'Now tell us all about the political happenings in U.K.'

A half hour passed in amiable conversation but I was a little disturbed at the lack of urgency. After all, they had not wasted any time getting me out to Zambia; now it seemed there was time to spare. I was going to be away from home for Christmas having made every effort to respond to the initial urgency. Later, with experience, I would allow for the Z factor in any plans I made. There seemed to be a lot of it about.

2

The Kafue River

At the hotel I made my way to my room on the first floor. In a long corridor I narrowly avoided a collision with a small boy who hurtled towards me, his feet clad in large mops, skating on the polished surface. So this was how the corridors maintained their high polish. I wrote my first airmail letter home, then went down to lunch. In the afternoon I explored a little. Cairo Road looked rather fine; a wide street with Jacaranda trees growing down a central area. Traders sat beneath their shade selling a variety of wares.

Back in my room I prepared to rest until dinner. A man bearing a flit spray appeared, to spray under my bed. At dinner I began to realise just how lonely one can feel surrounded by the noise and jollity of people with friends or family.

I had been happy with my room overlooking the street, but, with the windows open to let in some air and fly screens to keep out winged marauders, I was disturbed from time to time by the sound of fast driven cars, the squeal of tyres cornering on hot roads and the impatient honking of horns.

At breakfast next morning I was informed that a man was enquiring for me at the desk. I asked the messenger to conduct him to my table. Perhaps he would like some coffee. I might need an extra cup. After a few minutes a man approached. About forty years old I guessed; deeply tanned; no tenderfoot this one. He offered his hand. 'I'm Donald Hawksworth, Cattle Development, I'm a livestock officer.' We shook hands.

'Help yourself to coffee.'

'Thank you, I will.' Hawksworth poured coffee. 'Now then, Skottke and I between us own a boat on the Kafue river. I'm going over there now with my boy. It's Saturday, time to relax. If you've nothing better to do you might like to come along. Could be we might catch a fish or two. What do you say?'

'I have nothing better to do; in fact I have nothing at all to do. I'm with you and more than grateful.'

'Come as you are. It's the rainy season but if we get wet we will soon dry off.' He grinned. 'You'll need to get some shorts. Get your knees browned. White knees are a dead give away.'

The river was wide and slow moving. The boat sturdily built with a steel hull and outboard motor, the sun beat down on us, not a rain cloud in sight. 'It'll be cooler on the water,' said Hawksworth cheerfully as we manoeuvred the heavy boat into the river. 'We're sure to get some rain. Very welcome in this heat. Short sharp showers, very heavy but we'll be dried out again in fifteen minutes or so.'

With all aboard and afloat, Hawksworth's son, a boy of about eleven said, 'We won't go hungry, we have some sandwiches and a bag of mangoes. They grow in our garden. Oh, and a big flask of tea.'

'Sounds good,' I said. 'I expect you can tell me all about the wildlife we may see.'

'Not sure,' said the boy. 'I know a fish eagle, they have white necks and we are bound to run into hippos. There are crocodiles in the river but we don't see them very often.'

After about an hour, with black clouds gathering overhead we nosed into the bank. The rain when it came was a deluge, not of long duration but unbelievably heavy. The boat offered little in the way of shelter so we were thoroughly soaked. The rain stopped as suddenly as it had started and in the hot sunshine which followed we soon dried out. We decided to stay put for a time and Hawksworth tried his hand with the rod. His

boy meantime dispensed mangoes, sandwiches and tea. He seemed to have a good
appetite for mangoes and reduced the
contents of the bag considerably while his
father stood in the bows hoping for a catch.
After about half an hour Hawksworth hauled
out a catfish; an enormous, sluggish creature
which he returned to the river. 'Not very
palatable,' he said. Later we passed a nearly
naked man standing upright in a dugout
canoe, I guessed that any catfish he hooked
would end up in a pot.

Some way upstream we encountered
hippos. With a steel hulled boat, Hawksworth
was confident enough to go in close so that I
might get some photos. The hippos, well used
to river traffic, took little notice although
some mouths opened wide for the camera.
Unfortunately, despite our relative closeness,
my point-and-click camera yielded a photo of
hippo heads apparently at a distance. Much
further on, the river became even wider, so
wide indeed as to look more like a lake.

Hawksworth was looking at his watch.
'Time to go about, head for home, the sun
goes down soon after six. We should get the
boat out of the water before dark.'

With the boat safely beached we headed
back to Lusaka. The sun dropped rapidly to
the horizon and a glorious African sunset

enveloped us. A perfect way to end the day. As we parted Hawksworth said, 'Skottke knows you're here. He'll be round to sort things out with you; he has a lot on his plate, doesn't spare himself. You'll get on, I'm sure of that.'

I went up to my room. I had plenty to put in my letter. Hippos, fish eagles, a dugout canoe, a catfish all of thirty inches long, torrential rain, hot sun and a wonderful sunset. I didn't see much of Hawksworth thereafter. He being on the ranching side of things and me on pigs and farming, our paths just didn't cross but I was always grateful for that day on the river. I took on board for future action one piece of advice he had given me; to get myself a pair of shorts.

3

Visit to Nkumba

Sunday passed quietly. In the morning I explored, pinpointing different enterprises. African Farm Equipment (A.F.E.) selling, as the name implied, all sorts of farm requirements. Nearby was a large store where I might purchase some more suitable clothes: shorts, a shirt with plenty of pockets and knee-length white socks. I felt that kitted out and with a deepening of my tan and some careful attention to my white knees I might look the part. I thought that this shopping might occupy Monday morning but my plans changed after breakfast when, on enquiring at the desk if there was anything for me, I was handed a message from Skottke. He would call for me at 9am. I settled myself in the foyer to wait.

He arrived five minutes early. I took stock as he walked briskly across the foyer: medium height, 30's, fairish hair cropped short, tinted glasses and wearing what I was to learn was a safari suit, shorts and a light jacket, no shirt and of course the obligatory white knee-length socks and brown shoes. At the desk he said, 'Yes, I'm meeting a Mr Thomson.' The man behind the desk pointed. I was already on my way to meet him. We shook hands; he introduced himself, 'Martin Skottke. Well, we might as well be off,' he said, heading for the door.

I was hard put to it to keep up. This was a man in a hurry. 'Where are we going?' I managed.

'Out to the farm, chase up those painters, we can talk on the way.' His car was parked by the door. We headed off down Cairo Road. I could see he was unfazed by the chaotic traffic all around us. Everyone seemed to be in a desperate hurry. Horn blowing was the order of the day.

'You are well used to things here,' I remarked, 'Have you been here long?'

Skottke smiled briefly. 'Yes, long enough. I came to Africa when I was twenty, Southern Rhodesia. I worked for an English farmer, learned to speak English. Yes, later I was involved in setting up cattle auctions for villagers to sell their cattle.'

He concentrated on his driving as we joined the Great East Road, a well-surfaced dual carriageway. We passed through a small township. 'Chelston, your post office and shopping place. We turn off soon on to a dirt road. Twenty miles from Lusaka to the farm. Dirt roads will be a new experience for you.' Skottke grinned. 'You'll soon see.'

Rocketing along the dirt road, I said, 'You speak perfect English but I detect a slight accent which I can't place and you said you learned to speak English in Rhodesia.'

He laughed. 'I'm German, or more specifically I'm from Prussia. That was my home until the Russians chased us out and took over our country. I was eight years old at the time.' He was not to be drawn further on this. 'It's a long story,' was his reply to further questions. In fact it was many years later that I learned about the Russians entering his town, Königsberg, now Kaliningrad; the gunfire in the streets and the sad loss of his fifteen-year-old brother. It seemed that his brother was apprehended by Russian soldiers as he left school. Together with others of his age he was bundled into a truck and driven off presumably to a labour camp. Wherever he ended up he was not seen again despite efforts over many years to trace him. This was followed by the night time escape with his mother and father as they left pushing a few belongings and supplies on a handcart. Like many refugees they had a long trek; fraught with danger and hardship, across the breadth of Germany to become accommodated in the extreme west of Germany.

We were travelling at considerable speed, a large dust cloud billowing out behind. I was aware of the steep camber and a slight rippling of the surface. Conscious of my interest, Skottke smiled. 'The steep drop at the sides takes care of water when it rains. The surface is graded by big machines at intervals; it is best to drive fast; a smoother ride. You'll soon get used to all this, we pass a beer hall soon, best to give it a wide berth, it gets a bit rough.'

Soon we turned off on to a smaller dirt road. Skottke slowed to let a troupe of monkeys cross. 'They like the maize. Break down the stalks to get at the cobs, can make a lot of damage. Wild pigs also, they are even worse. You will be issued with a shotgun to discourage them.'

'What sort of pig buildings do we have?' I wanted to know. Skottke gave me a guarded look. 'How much do you know?'

'Well I was told at my interview that the buildings would all be in place.'

'We are nearly there,' he replied, turning down a track. 'Yes, you can see for yourself.' A few hundred yards on he stopped the car. We got out and passed through a gap in the trees. 'This is it, fifteen acres waiting to be developed.'

'But there is nothing here,' I managed. 'Just a lot of scrub trees. These will have to be removed, soil levelled, roads prepared and buildings put up . . .'

'A survey has been done. There is a contour map,' said Skottke.

I ignored the interruption ' . . . and water to find and electricity to sort out. A bit daunting.'

'This is Zambia,' said Skottke. 'This is how it is. Yes, we call it the Z factor, but now you are here I'm sure we can get this project moving.' He clapped me on the shoulder. 'Cheer up, we'll go and see your house now.'

I had begun to notice that he rather overused the word yes, often starting a sentence with it, the only slight flaw I could detect in his perfect grasp of English. We got back in the car; I still felt somewhat disturbed, there seemed to be too much of this Z factor about but I was somewhat reassured by Skottke's assurances. I felt I could rely on his support.

A short distance took us to the farm. A long open-fronted building housed tractors and machinery. My bungalow was nearby. An ancient truck stood outside. Inside, four men were at work. A large drum of slaked lime stood in the middle of the main room. This lime wash was being liberally brushed onto

21

the walls. This was a method I had used on the stables and byres in my younger days. Little care was being taken of floors, doors, or windows.

Skottke adopted a stern managerial manner. 'You will finish today,' he demanded.

'Ah no Bwana,' replied the painter. 'There is much work.'

'Tomorrow then or no pay.'

I listened and learned. 'And everything clean, no mess or no pay.'

Broad grins beamed our way then the activity resumed.

'I'll show you round,' said Skottke. 'This is the best of the housing and near the implement shed. The large concrete reservoir we passed can be used to irrigate your garden. It is filled from the borehole next to it. Yes, you will never be short of water.'

'What other houses are there?' I wanted to know.

'Two other houses. An old farmhouse with a grass thatched roof and another bungalow; not as new or as good as yours. The dirt road stops by the sheds but continues as a track to the houses, first the farmhouse then the bungalow — about 200 yards.'

My bungalow proved to be roomy with lino tiled floors throughout. The lounge ceiling was almost covered in greenery from a pot plant with foliage which crept across the width of the room to and fro, attached to the laths which supported the soft board cladding. Two good-sized bedrooms, a dining room, kitchen and scullery and a bathroom with a flush toilet completed a satisfactory living space.

Outside at the rear I came across an unusual structure.

'Rhodesian boiler,' explained Skottke. 'Gives you a hot water supply.'

I was intrigued by this apparently crude piece of equipment which proved to be extremely efficient. A dome-shaped open fronted structure housed a large fire basket over which two connected forty gallon drums rested on metal supports. Water was piped from a header tank and taken by gravity from the bottom of one of the drums to the hot water points in the house.

'Very efficient,' said Skottke. 'Yes, get a good heat going then push a tree trunk in. It will burn away slowly. Give it a nudge every day, it will keep you going for weeks.'

The structure of the house intrigued me. 'Built for the climate,' explained Skottke. 'The tin roof has a big overhang at the eaves. This shades walls and windows. It also allows airflow under the roof to keep the house cool. The ledge round the lower part of the walls is an ant course. Ants are not keen on walking upside down. All the windows are screened against insects. What do you think?'

'Well it's not home but very liveable.'

Our next stop was the compound in a clearing nearby. I looked around at the grass-thatched, mud-plastered huts. 'This is where the arable workers live; the huts are called Nyumbas. Yes, they can build a house in five days. There used to be cattle here, there's a borehole and a water trough.'

I turned to look at a long concrete trough, perhaps thirty feet long. It had obviously been filled with water as a few children were in it splashing and laughing. They became aware of us and watched wide-eyed over the concrete rim. As we approached they disappeared over the other side, wet bodies gleaming, and in a blizzard of white feet soles they scampered across the clearing to disappear among the trees. A few women appeared from the huts and grouped together to watch our departure.

'We'll find Samuel,' said Skottke. 'He's the arable Capitaal.'

'Zambian?' I queried. 'Yes Zambian, a good man, knows his job.'

Driving round wide headlands we at last came across Samuel. He was with a tractor and trailer loaded with bags of fertiliser. It seemed clear that he was servicing a fertilizer distributor which was travelling at considerable speed down the maize rows.

With introductions over I asked, 'How big is this field?' It was Skottke who answered. 'Yes, about two hundred acres.' Samuel filled me in with other information. 'We have six hundred acres of maize planted. Half before the rains started; half after.' Skottke explained further. 'The rains start in early November. If the rains are good the early planted maize gets a good start; if the rains fail it is bad news for the early planted stuff, so we hold back on half of it and wait for the rain then we plant what we have held back on. If the first lot has failed we replant after the rains have started. Yes, you can see how important a good rainy season can be.'

'We plough very deep, put lots of weight on the plough.' Samuel made a contribution to my information. 'This helps to soak up the rain.'

I had already noticed the large disc ploughs in the implement shed but Samuel had more to contribute. 'With good rains the maize grows fast. We have to get the fertilizer on before the maize gets too high for tractor work; then we would need an aeroplane.'

Skottke was nodding. 'We have aeroplanes for crop spraying, fertilizing, and the like.'

I felt I had a foot on a learning curve. There was much to get used to. On the way home Skottke had decided we ought to get together for a planning session. He suggested that I have two days to sort out my thoughts then I should come to his office for an all-day planning meeting.

Reflecting on the day, I thought I had been confronted in a big way by the Z factor. I was glad I had Skottke on board.

4

A Christmas Party

Approaching Kwacha House I almost bumped into Mr Kapota who had just left the building. He greeted me then said, 'Good news. Your vehicle will be ready in a day or so, you will have time to choose your furniture. You will need an L.P.O. book. Skottke will sort it out for you.'

'I'm heading for Mr Skottke's office now. There's a lot of planning to do and a budget to prepare.'

'Good, good,' said Mr Kapota. 'Take the lift, second floor, turn right out of the lift. Third door on the left. I have a meeting, must be off.'

My tap on the door was answered by a young female secretary. 'I'm Thomson,' I said, 'come to see Mr Skottke.' She smiled and silently ushered me in.

'Take a seat. Just a few things to get off the desk.' Skottke was obviously at the centre of much that went on. He spent ten minutes signing papers and putting things in baskets, then he was free. He called across to his secretary who was turning the pages of a magazine and obviously not busy. 'No telephone calls and no one through the door.'

'OK.' said the girl, 'I understand,' and she returned to her magazine.

Across the desk Skottke fixed me with a steely stare. Without his tinted glasses I could see his eyes were blue. 'You first,' he said.

'Questions?'

'Fire away.'

'What would you say average litter size would be?'

'Five,' said Skottke, grinning at my look of disbelief. 'Yes five, no more. Next question.'

'Why so few?'

Soon my worst fears had been confirmed. Breeding stock was of poor quality. No fresh blood had been introduced in living memory; there would be no experienced pig workers; there was a functioning feed mill in Lusaka but ingredients could be variable. I had already ruled out early weaning and I now mentally crossed out five week weaning and got back to an old fashioned eight weeks.

I had a clear vision of what I wanted. A large building to house stored grain and milling equipment; from this building a roadway would service the main stock housing. One side of the road would be developed first. Finishing units, a gap, then farrowing pens which would be adapted to serve as rearing pens when the sows were weaned and moved on to the service unit. The weaned pigs would move to the fattening housing when the pens were again needed for farrowing. My aim, having considered all the negatives, was to keep the operation simple and housing-use flexible. The first part of the building programme would handle 250 sows with a mirror image on the other side of the road also housing 250 sows.

A nucleus of breeding stock would have to be imported to produce commercial breeding sows. I had no intention of introducing pigs until we were building on the second phase. From experience I realised how quickly a pig population can grow. Once the sows were served piglets would appear about 114 days later and would soon need fattening accommodation. The process was unstoppable whereas a building plan could run into all sorts of problems. I had now become very aware of the Z factor.

I also had ideas about slurry drains and slurry disposal. I think Skottke was somewhat bemused by all this but interested and excited as well. Having listened carefully he made his contribution. 'We will be required to produce a budget. Would you like me to take that on board? I know what things cost; I know a commercial pig farmer down in Mazabuka who will have some idea what his building costs were. I think I can produce something they will accept upstairs. Once it's approved at Ministry level, yes we can get moving.'

I discovered something about Skottke from this meeting. He had little regard for food during the working day. I had expected a break for lunch but that didn't happen. By three o'clock I excused myself saying I would like to get back to the hotel to work on a building plan. I left with a local purchase order book which I could use instead of money, a list of items of furniture I was allowed to order from a nominated retailer and the name of a garage where I could collect my pick-up in two days' time.

'Yes, I'll work on the budget for a few days, then it will have to go before Mr Kalulu at the Ministry for Rural Development. It shouldn't take long, two weeks at most.'

Had he perhaps forgotten the Z factor?

★ ★ ★

Two weeks passed. There had been no word of the budget but I was at last installed in my newly whitewashed bungalow. Whoever had done the clean-up had done a good job; doors and windows had been scrubbed clean,

the floors had been polished and my new
Toyota pick-up rested in the attached garage.
The furniture I had chosen had been
delivered and arranged. I was happy with the
result.

Another week passed and Skottke visited.
'Nothing approved yet and time is passing.'

'It's very frustrating,' I agreed. 'What if I
got on and cleared the site?'

'What if you got on and built the thing?
Could you do it?' I thought this over. The
alternative didn't appeal. Getting quotes from
builders with no pig knowledge, waiting for
those, waiting for decisions as they are
considered, waiting — waiting. I didn't think
I could stand it. 'Yes I can do it.'

I took stock of my credentials in this
direction. I had rattled a surveyor's chain
round Blythswood Square while attending
agricultural college in Glasgow. Here I had
also done a bit with the dumpy level. I
understood about angles of elevation. On one
farm I had been involved in developing a pig
unit including planning and supervising the
building work. On others I had laid concrete
floors to levels and had some block and bricklaying experience. My welding skills were not
great but I had been known to stick things
together.

'I'll back you all the way,' Skottke seemed

relieved, 'You'll need a bulldozer, that's roads department; the electricity board is in Lusaka, there's some department at the ministry that finds boreholes. You'll soon find your way around.'

'How do I get labour?'

'Just tell your arable boys and labour will turn up. You will need a lorry to haul materials; I will take you to a Mercedes dealer. There's Castcrete who make concrete blocks; a timber yard,' Skottke paused for breath. 'Yes, and I nearly forgot. We are invited to a pre-Christmas party. This includes you. You will go with us. Come to my place, I will give you directions; you will meet the manager of the feed company, a good friend.'

'But when is this party?'

'Tonight,' said Skottke. 'Short notice. I hope you had not made other arrangements?'

'Hardly,' I said. 'Just let me have the directions.'

While Skottke jotted down the information he said, 'Get the Christmas and New Year shut down out of the way and you can start putting yourself about.' I watched his departing dust cloud. I was glad I wouldn't now have the hassle of looking for local contractors, collecting tenders, getting a starting date, trying to explain what I needed, coping with delays. It was now up to me, I was more than ready to put myself about.

★ ★ ★

I was a bit apprehensive about the party. What to wear? Would I feel out of it being a new boy with no African experience? But arriving at the Skottkes' home I was immediately made to feel welcome. Skottke introduced me to his wife. 'This is Lesley, you won't have trouble with her accent, yes, she's English.'

Lesley came forward smiling. 'But I was born in India and spent much of my life in Africa married to a German. I don't know what that might have done to my accent.'

'I'm hardly in a position to judge, I'm Scottish.' I was beginning to feel more relaxed. 'I wasn't sure what to wear. This is new ground for me.' Lesley looked me over. 'Slacks and a shirt, I think you'll pass. What do you think, Martin?'

Martin was wearing a safari suit with a cravat and long trousers. 'Yes you'll do. Some will dress up a bit, some will be wearing shorts and a bush shirt. A cravat is useful, some hotels won't let you in for dinner unless you have a tie or cravat.'

'I have a tie in my pocket.'

33

'You won't need it, we are going to Martin Perkin's house not far away and, yes, I think I told you he runs the feed mill. It's owned by one of your big British companies. I want you to meet him.'

The party was under way when we arrived. Dress was varied as Skottke had suggested. Many wore shorts, cravats were in evidence but the ladies had dressed up, wearing cocktail dresses or pretty summer frocks. Drinks were plentiful and food, some of it unfamiliar to me, was delicious. Conversation flowed easily and there was considerable interest in my project. Martin Perkins put me in the picture as regards his mill products; no early weaning feed, sow meal composition often changing due to scarcities of one ingredient or another, long haulage distances, unpredictable rains, crop failures. 'If they ever close the border, which could happen, we can say goodbye to fish meal,' he said. I was glad I had opted for late weaning and for milling our own feed.

Sated with food and mellowed with wine, we left around midnight. A three-quarter moon lit our way as we approached the house to be greeted by a large dog which had been patrolling the garden.

'Great Dane?' I queried.

'With a bit of Rhodesian Ridgeback,'

34

agreed Skottke. 'He's a great guard dog. Killed a snake in the garden one day.'

'Venomous?'

'Green Mamba, yes, one of the bad ones.'

I shivered at the thought of snakes in the garden.

As I took my leave, Lesley said, 'After the holiday we'll have you over for dinner. Is a Saturday night alright?'

'I shall have to check my diary,' I joked. 'Yes, a Saturday night would be perfect, I'll look forward to it.'

★　★　★

Everything shut down for the Christmas and New Year holiday. This was a bad time to have what we now call deep vein thrombosis but I was fated to spend an uncomfortable time with a grossly swollen leg, turgid and painful. I had no idea what was wrong with it and didn't know whether it was better to sit with my leg resting or to be out on the site pegging out. During this period my thoughts drifted homewards. I imagined what they were doing. Were they missing me as much as I was missing them? Idleness does not help to combat misery so I spent more time on the site and after the holiday I set off to Lusaka to find a doctor. I saw a forthright Scotsman who delivered a strongly worded lecture on thrombosis and its attendant dangers and I left with his warnings ringing in my ears and a course of blood thinning tablets. They seemed to do the trick and I was soon fully recovered.

★ ★ ★

After the break I started making calls. At the Electricity Board I found a rather world-weary Englishman in charge. I explained my project and the need for a 3-phase supply.

The man thought things over, then with a tired grin said, 'You have a job on out there. It won't be plain sailing. Now let's see. You have a single phase supply at the moment. We would have to bring in a new supply. It would mean a lot of poles.'

'When can you start?'

'In due course,' he said. 'You are not in U.K. now. You can't expect everything done yesterday.' He held out his hand. 'But I wish you the best of luck.' He didn't exactly add, you'll need it, but I felt it was implied. It was to be some months before I saw poles marching slowly across country towards our site.

At the roads department an Indian manager agreed to send a bulldozer in a few days. At Castcrete I was given tea and a ready ear by the manager, Ben Van Kuringen, a cheerful Dutchman, who intimated that he would be delighted to have the business; he could supply blocks, slabs, whatever we needed. He gave me a number for Chilanga Cement and the use of his phone. He put me in touch with a timber yard, a steel stockholder and A.F.E. (African Farm Equipment). I alerted all these to our needs. Ben kept me well supplied with concrete blocks and later, concrete slabs. We became good friends.

Back at the farm, Samuel told me that there was sand on one of the other farms (Zambia Dairy Development) and I was able to confirm that this was river sand, white, soft and suitable for bricklaying mortar.

Things were shaping up; I needed to trigger the bush telegraph. I explained my needs to Samuel: bricklayers, carpenters, welders, labourers. I also suggested we would need Nyumbas to house them. Samuel thought this over. 'Me and my men can build a few Nyumbas; bricklayers, carpenters, ah no Bwana, they want to work in town. Labourers, plenty will come. You show them Bwana, they soon learn.'

'You mean I have to train them to lay blocks, to do welding, to put on roofs?'

'They learn quick, Bwana. You see.'

37

* * *

The bulldozer was on site as promised and was busy clearing trees and levelling sites for the buildings. I left a few trees, that were not in the way of my building plans, to provide shade and add to landscaping which might follow the building. I had another plan for the bulldozer. I found a site away from the pig buildings and not too far from the compound. Here I pegged out a regulation size football pitch. I had begun to realize that with everything done with pick and shovel I would end up with a lot of families in the compound. I guessed that the young men would like to play and others would enjoy watching. In any case I still liked to kick a ball about. When the bulldozer man had finished on the site I set him to work on the football field; his brief, to create a smooth level surface. I was delighted with the result. Grass didn't matter, a level dirt pitch was fine. In the evening my first site worker arrived. I saw him just as the sun was setting; he was loitering by my garden gate. I went out to him.

'I want work,' he said.

I looked him over. He could have been a bushman from the Kalahari or a pigmy from the Congo. He was less than five feet tall, slightly built. 'Are you strong?' I asked.

He smiled broadly. 'Too much, Bwana.'

I was to learn that this was a favourite expression, often used inappropriately.

'Come to the farm buildings at six in the morning,' I said. 'Where will you sleep?'

'Is OK. Bwana. I sleep somewhere.'

'Samuel is building Nyumbas, when they are ready you can have one.'

'OK. Bwana. My name is Pondani.'

This was the start of a steady stream of workers. Soon they caught up with Samuel's building efforts. It was his suggestion that new workers should build their own Nyumbas. 'It takes only five days. Supply a tractor and trailer to collect wood and grass. If you pay them to do this they are happy.'

How very simple life could be. Somewhere to live in five days. I took the opportunity of observing the method. First a palisade of stakes driven in to form a square. Then the roof timbers lashed together at the top to form a pointed roof and secured to the walls with strips of bark. The bark of a particular tree was used which lent itself to being cut into long unbroken strips. The strips had been soaked overnight and used wet so that as they dried out in the sun the lashings tightened. The framework was now securely held together. All that remained was to thatch the roof with elephant grass and plaster the gaps in the wall stakes with mud. This dried hard in the sun.

And so the Nyumbas grew in numbers; families arrived, the compound came alive with the sound of children playing, cook fires twinkled in the evening and a sizeable number of men assembled by the farm buildings at six each morning. I had to keep a register for payment purposes and, rather like a schoolmaster, called out the unfamiliar names; Sunday, Iron, Cobra, Petrol, Gotson, and some English names, Joseph, Samuel, John, Simon. We worked through till 2pm, no breaks, which left four hours before sunset for the young men to employ their leisure as they saw fit. Some might take their catapults and go hunting kalulu — rabbits to my mind, except that they lived above ground like our hares — or they might go digging for field rats, yes rats for the cook pot, or setting snares for birds, collecting caterpillars, sometimes chopping down a tree to get at them, and edible vegetables such as wild spinach and any edible berries. This to supplement a diet of mealie meal (maize porridge) and kapenta (small dried fish) cooked on fires outside the Nyumbas as night closed in.

A one-meal a day regime meant that there was no obesity. The men on the site were lean and fit; the women, hewers of wood for the fires and carriers of water from the borehole were equally slim and strong. Neck muscles which had been developed since childhood enabled them to carry heavy loads on their heads. A five-gallon drum was the favoured utensil for water carrying. Men were not trained in this skill, neck muscles were not therefore so developed. It was not uncommon to see a woman, a child slung on her back and a large bundle on her head with her husband ahead of her unencumbered. I was often impressed to see a large basket of eggs weaving its way along a crowded street or a rolled umbrella being transported likewise. This expertise encouraged a good posture and a measured tread.

5

The Postal Strike

I had established a Post Office box at Chelston and letters were passing to and fro with reasonable frequency. Then the blow fell. It came out of the blue. A postal strike. For the first time U.K. postal workers were on strike. It lasted seven weeks.

Without contact with home I felt cut adrift; I could only imagine how Renee was feeling. It was the 20th January 1971. I had hardly had time to get myself settled into my project. I had to do something; this was a situation that was making me unhappy and worried. Someone suggested I contact the British High Commission.

I did better than this. I presented myself at the reception desk where a kind, motherly lady listened to my tale of woe and then sat thinking. Finally she looked up.

'Who is your M.P. back home?'

'Jeremy Thorpe.'

'Hm, I have an idea.'

'Go on,' I said, 'can my M.P. help?'

'Oh yes, I think he can.' She handed me

paper and an envelope. 'Just write to Jeremy, explain your problem, ask him to contact your wife. Address it to Jeremy Thorpe at the House of Commons, Westminster. I will pop it in the diplomatic bag.'

'Will he reply?'

'Oh yes, come back in a few days and see if anything has come back.'

Four days later the diplomatic bag produced a letter from Jeremy Thorpe. He had telephoned my wife; she was fine and he had reassured her as to my welfare. He also informed me that he would check on things at his end from time to time and let me know if there was a problem.

Jeremy Thorpe, before his life spiralled downwards, was a diligent M.P. In particular he was a good constituency M.P. Very visible. He could be seen on occasion talking to stall holders in Barnstaple's Pannier market. Always approachable, he had a wonderful memory for names. I recall an occasion when he was electioneering, travelling round Devon's many small villages. He arrived in our village; the car pulled up, Jeremy leapt out, microphone in hand and soon was addressing a group of villagers. He would break off to greet a new arrival. 'Hello Bert, nice to see you, how's the allotment doing?' Then, full of energy, he would be back into his spiel. When he had finished he shook hands here and there, always with, it seemed, a name. 'Let's see, Thomas isn't it? If I remember rightly you work at . . . ' And so it went on. His sad fall from grace was still some way ahead.

One day there was a letter for me in the diplomatic bag. Jeremy Thorpe would be visiting Zambia where he had business interests. This I already knew from the kind lady at the reception desk. He would be staying at the Inter Continental Hotel. We could meet up for a chat; he gave me a date and a time. This seemed to be a good idea; I wrote an acceptance note for the return bag.

I attended as agreed, reported to the reception desk and was informed that Mr Thorpe was busy with the chairman of the company where his interests lay. Would I wait? He would be down shortly. I waited, an hour passed, then a further fifteen minutes. Outside the sun was on its downward journey. We were at the peak of the rains. I had already experienced difficult driving conditions. I left a message to say that because of the possible state of the roads, I had to leave.

The telephone was no help in a situation like this. Calls to outside Zambia had to be booked. Unreliable at the best of times it could be days before your slot came up.

Ten to one you would not be near the telephone when, or indeed if, a call was offered to you.

Seven weeks seemed a long time passing, but eventually the strike was over, letters could pass between us again. It was a great relief to me and to the family back home.

6

The Water Diviner

Now I had enough labour for two small working parties. Road making occupied one group while the others made a start on digging foundations. I soon realised I would need a lot more men for all the hand digging. The lorry was now on site and I needed a lorry driver. I put the word out, labourers arrived most days and a lorry driver soon put in an appearance. I tested his driving skills; he seemed competent, then the interview. 'Your name?'

'John Tembo.'

'Are you working somewhere else?'

'Yes Bwana.' He named a Danish project which was operating about twenty miles away. They ran a dairy farm and trained young Africans. I had visited them and they had been very helpful. Indeed when I had mentioned my need for a level of some sort they sent me off with a Kern Quickset on indefinite loan.

'I must speak to them.'

'Ah Bwana I no work there now. I finish.'

'You have told them?'

'Yes Bwana I come work for you.'

'OK. you can start.' My need for a lorry driver was rather pressing. 'But I will talk to them.'

★ ★ ★

About this time I began to realise that some of my recruits were coming from my neighbour's farm. I had no wish to antagonise my closest neighbour so I paid a visit. I arrived in early afternoon. My knocking set dogs barking and after a short delay a lady came to the door. A tall handsome woman, she greeted me with a pleasant smile.

She had a South African accent and I was to learn later that she was from South Africa but born of English parents. 'I'm Diane Nel,' she said, 'can I help you?'

'I'm from the farm next door,' I said, 'I would like a few words with you and your husband if that is convenient.'

'I'll get my husband,' she said, 'he's in bed.'

I waited. A man appeared, tanned, forties, stocky, wearing shorts, shirt and socks. He smiled and shook hands. 'I'm Christie Nel, come in. I'm pleased to see you.'

'I'm sorry to disturb you. Are you ill?'

He looked at me uncomprehendingly for a

moment, then laughed. 'No, no, just having a nap. You'll find a lot of farmers have a nap after lunch.'

I was still on a learning curve. I explained my mission.

'Can you name any of them?' he asked.

'Well there's one called Iron.'

'Yes, he worked here. He understands gardening. We do a bit of market gardening here, get him to do your garden.'

Mrs Nel invited me to supper. 'Come over about eight, we'll have supper and get to know each other better.' This was the start of many such evenings and so we became good friends and neighbours. Diane was the soul of hospitality. When Renee called for the first time she was to sample this hospitality and friendship.

'You must be Renee from Nkumba,' she had said. 'I could tell you were European, there are not too many around here. Come in, we'll have some coffee and a chat.'

Later we sometimes did business. When a fire swept through one of Christie's maize fields when I was in my final year and had pigs to feed I bought this damaged grain, blackened but still useable. We agreed a price and shook hands. 'Just collect the bags off the field, man. Let me know how many you have.' I found all this very refreshing.

Road making was going on apace. The method was simple enough. The road was shaped up using a tractor rear-mounted grader blade. The surface was covered with a thin layer of latherite, a flaky sort of gravel which had excellent binding properties. We were lucky enough to have a seam of this on the edge of the site. Tractor traffic soon rolled the latherite into a hard wearing surface and of course roads could be graded and tidied up as required.

Trench digging was making progress as more workers arrived. The first requirement was to dig out trenches on either side of a fattening building — our first target — to accommodate the slurry drainage system. This system worked using only gravity and as such required steep falls which on some sites would have meant a lot of deep digging. Our site had favourable contours which would save excessive digging but meant that the building had to be made up where the site fell away. While this meant more walling and filling I could see a benefit in the raised end of the building; we had a ready-made loading point at lorry level when we started to market pigs.

Plenty of good hard stone was available where someone in a past era had tried his hand at mining for copper. Deep in the bush a tunnel had been dug into a small hill. The ground around the entrance was littered with rocks from the excavation. No one could give me any history of this dig. I explored the tunnel, much of the rock had the green seams of copper, but all I found was a pair of nesting barn owls. The tunnel came to a dead end some thirty yards in. Another source of hard filling was a roofless tobacco barn on the farm which we could demolish for an ample supply of brick rubble.

I had been given an assistant; a young African called Peter, who, despite having attended an Agricultural College and having been sent on training schemes to Denmark and U.K. proved to have no aptitude for, or knowledge of, either arable farming or building work. I therefore decided to promote one of the men on the site to the role of foreman, to assist me with taking levels, pegging out and checking the work. My choice was a personable young man called Sunday. He spoke very reasonable English, had worked at one time as a storeman in Lusaka, could drive the pick-up to move materials on the site and seemed to grasp what the job was all about. He proved to be a good choice.

Soon another assistant arrived to help on the arable side. He had been recruited in

Tanzania. His name was Mahdi Welgi, an African-born Asian of Indian extraction. He arrived with his wife Yasmin and moved into the farm's other bungalow. Peter and family lived in the old farmhouse nearby.

Mahdi had benefited from agricultural training and employment. Aged twenty-eight and with considerable experience I could see he would be an asset to the enterprise and so it proved.

The Nyumbas in the compound were increasing day by day as more and more workers arrived. The final total was sixty, providing some ninety site workers. I was delighted when someone arrived who had some experience of bricklaying. Soon another bricklayer arrived. These two would train others when block laying started.

When walling and floor laying started we would need water on site. A team of Government surveyors came out to look for possible borehole sites. Their method was to assess the geological formation most likely to yield water. This they did by bouncing signals off the rocks below. I suggested they might start prospecting from the site outwards. They disagreed and explored some more distant terrain, finally marking two drilling points. I had the drilling contractors in but unfortunately science had let us down; both

51

drillings proved to be duds. It was Christie Nel who came to my rescue. He had an elderly uncle who found wells by water divining. Somewhat sceptical I decided to give it a go and one morning an elderly man appeared on the site.

'I've come to sort out your water,' he said. His accent spoke of South Africa.

'I understand from Christie you have had a lot of success.'

He smiled. 'A hundred percent so far. I hope you are not going to spoil my record.'

'I certainly hope not, we need the water.'

'Where do you want it?' he asked.

'Right here on the site.'

I marked out an area at the high side of the site where we should start. The man produced a sturdy forked maple twig and started moving about the marked area. After about ten minutes the twig pointed downwards indicating water and excitement made my heart beat faster. This was hopeful.

'Tie a knot in the long grass just here man,' he said.

I did so and he moved off criss-crossing the marked area. 'Here,' he called and another knot was tied. After two hours the knotted grass formed a distinct line. 'A stream down there sure enough. I will try for another.'

Soon he found another stream and glory

be, it ran into the first one well inside my marked area. We marked the spot with a stake driven securely.

'There's a lot of water down there man, could be deep, send for the drillers.'

I had always been a bit sceptical about water divining and I asked if I might try my hand. I soon found I did not have the gift as the twig never moved. The old man laughed. 'Let me show you man.' He took the twig. 'Now hold my hands, make sure they don't move. Now we will step over to the line we have marked and see what happens.'

As we straddled the line the twig started to move downwards. I had the man's hand firmly held. The twig would not be denied. It continued to move towards the water far below, stripping the bark to do so.

★　★　★

It took a few weeks to get the drilling rig back. I made sure they drilled on the exact imprint of the stake. The drill found some hard strata on its way down. The work was slow as the drill laboured in places but at last they were down two hundred feet. Heads were being shaken. It was beginning to look like another dud. 'Go another ten feet.' I was unwilling to admit defeat. They started drilling again and about half an hour later I heard shouts. They had found water, lots of it; several hours of pumping saw no reduction in the flow. It was a sustainable source. The output measured sixty gallons per hour. We had water in abundance and right on site.

I did not see the water diviner again but I asked Christie Nel to get a message to him — his record was intact. We had a borehole yielding sixty gallons per hour, a wonderful piece of work.

7

Lamek

With block laying about to commence I had some difficulty explaining to my two bricklayers that what we were starting with was a slurry drain not a house. They were at a loss.

'But Bwana, we always start at the corners.'

I tried with pencil and paper and careful description to get the plan understood. After a time I realised that it was impossible for them to grasp the concept of a steeply falling drain using gravity, with baffles creating turbulence to keep the solids in suspension. There would be slats over, to form a dunging passage; the outer wall would continue up to waist high and roof supports would extend upwards to support the roof. 'I will tell you what to do, you do what I say, OK., Choose a daka boy each. (to provide the bricklayer with blocks, mortar etc.) We have a cement mixer on site, Sunday will decide who works it.'

And so building work got under way. All

the materials were now to hand. The foundations had been laid in the trenches, block walls were started. The mixer man was getting to grips with his job. The bricklayers had to build level walls from a sloping base, but they were grinning happily now, shouting orders at their daka boys. Things were beginning to hum.

I was concerned that we had no dry store for the cement which was temporarily held in the tractor shed so I took a few helpers and we built a cement store. A wood framed building, corner posts anchored in the ground, corrugated iron cladding and a secure door which I padlocked at night. We also erected a barbed wire fenced yard with a gate, to offer some security for stored timber, corrugated sheeting and the like.

★ ★ ★

Sunday was doing a sterling job keeping an eye on things and helping me to communicate. With some seventy dialects in Zambia it was lucky that most understood Chinyanja as well as, in most cases, rudimentary English. One day Sunday approached me to report that one of the recruits was not up to the heavy digging.

'This man has been a house-boy Bwana. A

very nice man and he knows house work. You should have a house-boy Bwana.'

I had to agree. I had thought I could look after myself but soon realised that the demands of my job needed my full attention. 'Send him up to the house after work. What's his name?'

'His name is Lamek. He will look after your house well.'

And so Lamek became a part of my household. He kept my floors well polished; washed and pressed my clothes; made sure my brown shoes were up to scratch when I went to town and smiled his way through the days, ever cheerful, never grumbling. He moved, with his family into a house just beyond my garden. He had a small plot of land to grow some maize and seemed happy with his lot.

With my domestic chores, apart from cooking, taken over by Lamek, I took stock of my garden. There was a line of pawpaw trees, bananas at the bottom of the garden with Lamek's patch just beyond; an avocado tree grew just outside, together with a clutch of mangoes. Outside my back door a bush bore a type of hooded gooseberry and another coffee beans. I had Iron look it over.

'We can irrigate by making ditches for the water,' he said, 'then we can grow all the year, tomatoes, peppers, eggfruit, potatoes in two crops. We need seeds.'

I gave him a free hand, provided seeds as required and left him to get on with it. Seedlings I noted had to be protected from the hot sun in the early stages. This, Iron did by erecting a twig structure to carry a grass roof about two feet above the seed bed. Given plenty of water everything grew apace. Soon I had an abundance of good things. With the reservoir so close it was easy to unscrew the drainage stopcock and let water flow down the irrigation ditches.

Local telephone calls were very much hit or miss. I shared a line with other subscribers. If the bell gave out three short and one long it was for me; three longs was Christie Nel and so on. The children at one home would sometimes pick up the phone, say hello, giggle and pass it round to siblings. It was sometimes impossible to get past this children's playtime. On the other hand I might be trying to ring Christie Nel and someone recognising the Nel code would come on and the following conversation might ensue.

'Hello are you trying to get Christie?'

'Yes I am.'

'Well man, he's not at home. He's gone down south for a few days.'

'Would Diane have gone with him?'

'Yes, we believe so. Can we help you in any way.'

'No, not really. But thanks for letting me know.'

Needless to say this phone was out of order for long spells.

8

Unwelcome Visitors

With the arrival of our 3-phase electricity supply and power points ready for use I was aware of a need for a workshop. On my next visit to town I purchased a welding kit and suitable rods. A training exercise would be needed here. A pen of the fattening house was given over to workshop duties. Two work benches with vices were installed. Sheet metal, piping and U-section and angle iron were stacked outside. The job of the workshop would be to supply gates, gate hangings, water tanks and farrowing crates and perhaps much more.

I had been watching one young man named Joseph. He shared Pondani's surname of Daka. Joseph had shown an interest in the tractors and implements; I approached him with a proposal.

'I need someone to learn to weld and take charge of the workshop.'

I saw his eyes light up. 'Thank you, thank you Bwana. I learn very quick.'

'You will need helpers.'

He named some.

'I will get Sunday to come and talk to you. We need yourself and three others. OK.?'

My plan was to get all the component parts cut to size and stored so that assembly could start to fit in with the building programme. Gates and gate hangings were our first concern.

With the slurry channels in place the first fattening house began to take shape. The two daka boys had moved on to laying blocks under the eyes of the two senior bricklayers. I was amazed at how quickly people picked up new skills. The two apprentices now had a daka boy each to shout at. When roofing was about to start I had business in town so I instructed Peter and left him in charge. I put a line along where the lower sheet had to come to, giving a generous overhang to keep out the sun and I explained to Peter how he must, because of the overlap sideways and downwards of the top sheet, make constant small adjustments or the bottom line would grow.

On my return I discovered that the roof had grown well beyond the line which I had put up. The sheets had to be removed. I put Sunday in charge and the job went smoothly. Sunday had not had the advantages of training but his mind was quick and receptive. He was soon competent at all the jobs on the site whether it be laying concrete floors to levels or nailing up roof trusses. He helped me measure up and peg out the buildings. Soon he learned how to use the Kern Quickset and could at a pinch have taken levels.

Assembly of gates was now under way. Component parts were already prepared of course; lengths of angle iron equal to the four sides of a gate had been cut, notched at the corners and bent round to form a square which would be welded at the corner seams to make a frame and filled in with expamet mesh. Gate hangings were also being manufactured and were already built in to the first fattening house walls.

Welding skills had to be learned in the first instance of course. I was no expert. I had done little repair jobs on farms where I had worked but did not lay claims to being a serious welder. However I had read the booklet and knew enough to teach if not by example. I had started one to one with Joseph. I explained about shielding his eyes and the problems that could occur if this was not done. Next we moved to the control knobs on the appliance. I soon realised that degrees and other markings meant little to Joseph so I simplified by describing the controls as big fire and little fire; with big fire he should use the fat rods; with little fire he should use thin rods.

I demonstrated by joining two off cuts of flat steel together. Next having underlined safety, I left him to practise on a collection of offcuts. I had in mind to ask Christie Nel over to inspect Joseph's efforts but not before Joseph had had a chance to get to grips with it.

Later in the day I inspected Joseph's work. He seemed to be getting the hang of it and the welds were getting better.

'Tomorrow we will make a gate and get Christie Nel to check our work.'

Christie had a spell working in a garage in his young days. I had seen him weld things on his farm. I guessed that if he could repair machines he must be a competent welder.

The next day we did make a gate. Christie came over, smacked our work with a hammer and said, 'Not bad.' He spent the next two hours with Joseph refining his technique.

★   ★   ★

With one fattening house finished and the next well on its way I thought it prudent to set on a night-watchman. One young man volunteered and started his night patrols. He had nothing to report for several weeks but one evening I answered my door to urgent hammering. The night watchman stood there, obviously shaken. 'Bwana, Bwana,' he shouted, 'men are stealing.'

I calmed him down. 'How many?'

'Three or four. One has a shotgun.'

This was serious. I collected Mahdi from his house. By the time we reached the site they had gone. I talked it over with Mahdi. 'They'll be back,' he said.

I decided on a plan of action. The tyre marks of their truck showed that they had pulled up by the cement store but had not been able to force an entry. Some corrugated sheets or a piece or two of timber might have been taken. My plan was to puncture their vehicle in the first instance. I drove some six inch nails through some planks and arranged them buried in the dust between the gate and the cement store.

After darkness had fallen, Mahdi, myself and the night watchman drove to the site with lights off. We stationed ourselves at the top of the rise with a clear view of the storage area. I had not yet been issued with my shotgun, we were armed with pick handles, prepared to attack, lights fully on, horn blowing, shouting war cries from open windows.

The night-watchman was huddled under a

blanket in the back; after about an hour Mahdi was fast asleep and snoring loudly. It looked as though I had the night watch. By three in the morning I was angry enough to crack a few heads with my pick handle but none appeared. I retrieved my nail traps and I drove my drowsy passengers home.

The next night we were too tired to mount guard. The night-watchman reported hearing noises and some corrugated sheets appeared to have been taken. And so it went on. If we were on guard nothing happened. If we were asleep in our beds some pilfering went on.

I went to our local police station. They agreed to put someone on guard in the cement store. He would be armed. He would arrive in plain clothes, live in the compound and appear to be one of the workers. I expected him to be infiltrated into the compound in some secrecy, perhaps after dark. In the event he arrived while it was still light, in a Land Rover full of uniformed police. Everyone in the compound would know that the young man with the holstered revolver was a policeman. If the thieves were acting on information supplied from the compound, this seemed to defeat the object of the exercise.

For a week the policeman — probably terrified — slept in the cement shed. The word must have gone out about the revolver. The pilfering stopped. It was soon after that I was issued with a single-barrelled shotgun. I made sure it was seen; Lamek knew I kept it in a wardrobe. Some days I had it propped up in my pick-up. Mahdi could be heard scaring monkeys off the crop with it. Word would have gone out that we were armed. No doubt this was also a deterrent. I put it about that any form of stealing or supplying information to thieves from outside would mean instant dismissal. We were not troubled thereafter.

★   ★   ★

Another fattening house was nearly finished. It helped that all the walls were waist high. It also helped that we now had four men laying blocks with two daka boys showing signs of moving up. Block laying was most important as this had to be done before floors could be laid. Sunday could lead a team to lay floors and do the timber work and sheeting of roofs. All sawn timber had to be creosoted against the ravages of termites. Only gum poles were proof against these scavengers who could feed on anything, be it paperwork in your office, should they gain access, or your jacket should you be careless enough to leave it in the field. They seemed to be everywhere; a dead animal could be towed into the bush to be stripped to the bones in short order. I had no plans to store the present, rapidly ripening, harvest but I intended to have the mill up and ready to store the next crop. Milling equipment would have to be imported. I settled for a blending mill. The ingredients would be metered from their storage bins into a conveyor which would feed the hammer mill with grain as well as everything else. It would emerge from the hammer mill as a balanced ration ready to be fed to the pigs. I gave the order for this to a firm in Lusaka called Trans Continental Supplies. George Kalman, the owner, took the order and said, 'I hope you have allowed some time for this to get to you. It will come from Denmark by sea and as you are aware we are a long way from a port.'

'I think I have allowed for all that and while we're at it you had better get me some grain-moving augers.'

'Easier, they will come from U.K.'

I hoped it would all be in place by next harvest. The mill building would be large and high. I hoped to have it done fairly early in my second year.

★   ★   ★

67

The maize was tasselled and would soon be ripening. There was not much arable work until harvest started. Mahdi's men were clearing some more bush or doing maintenance jobs on the machinery. The rains had been good and the crop looked promising. Much of the rain seemed to fall at night — torrential — sometimes accompanied by a storm, almost continuous lightning, deafening thunder, a sight to behold but not pleasant under a tin roof. The work on the site was not much troubled by rain storms, which might last an hour, deliver two inches of rain, stop suddenly to be followed by hot sunshine. The earth would steam and everything would dry quickly. However, although the rains were tailing off, we could not be sure the rainy season was over till perhaps the end of May or even into the start of June. Harvest would be gathered by hand although we had been promised the use of a combine for the following year. With everything so far depending largely on manpower I looked forward to this move towards mechanisation.

9

Stick Dancing

Mahdi had settled in well and although he and Yasmin had a modern day approach to their religion, they regularly attended the Mosque in Lusaka and soon had many friends. Their particular form of Muslim worship had as its head the Aga Khan. He was the Father of their sect and events in his family were celebrated. The birth of a child to Ali Khan's wife was just such an event.

This called for a party. Mahdi asked me if a party at his bungalow would be in order.

'Of course,' I said. 'As long as I am invited.'

'Of course you are invited. We'll introduce you to stick dancing, goat meat and rice, Indian music, you'll meet a lot of people.'

'Stick dancing. It sounds like Morris dancing without the bells.'

'We'll need some short sticks,' said Mahdi.

I had a thought. 'Tell you what, we have lots of off-cuts in the workshop. Bits of metal pipe. We could sort through that lot.'

'Great,' said Mahdi, 'it will sound like a real battle.'

The party started outside where we had strung lights. People arrived bearing contributions to the feast. Perhaps about forty people turned up. The older guests sat on the most comfortable chairs. Some even managed to sit cross-legged in the restricted space of an armchair. The younger people sang, played music and danced.

I was dragged into the stick dancing. This involved an intricate pattern of prancing numbers. I took my cue from the person in front and I think I acquitted myself fairly well. At least I didn't damage anyone's fingers and kept my own intact.

With the party at its height I slipped off to my own bungalow. I went to sleep with the sound of steel on steel and the enthusiastic cries of the participants.

Football practice had become a feature of the afternoon free hours. I had given Peter the task of encouraging this with a view to getting a team together to play a few fixtures with schools and the like. I provided a football and observed emerging talent.

Peter was a useful performer and knew the rules. Sunday emerged as a centre forward. Tall, he could head goals and was agile and quick in the penalty box. There were several useful contenders for the goalkeeping spot and plenty with natural running speed. All could thump the ball with their bare feet.

Eventually a team emerged. A lot of coaching was needed to instil discipline and teamwork but they came around to staying in position and passing the ball.

I asked the Danish people up the road to get a team together to test our metal. I suggested a date some way ahead as I thought that training for a fixture would concentrate our players' minds.

I then began to think of kit. I wrote to Matt Busby at Manchester United to explain our situation and enquiring what happened to discarded kit at the famous club. I had a pleasant letter back written on Red Devils notepaper and signed by the great man. He was sorry, they had many such requests and couldn't support them all but wished us luck.

I then turned my mind to procuring kit by other means. It would have been easy to purchase shorts and jerseys and hand them out but I didn't want myself or the Company to be seen as benefactors; much better I thought if everyone could feel involved. I had a scheme in mind. I had the line of pawpaw trees; I didn't need them all but it was not easy to give them away equably. None had been stolen. I now offered the pawpaws for sale at a very small price. Lamek was in charge of sales and put the money in a pot on the mantelpiece. I doubt if I collected enough for the kit I purchased; ten yellow T-shirts, a white one for the goalkeeper and eleven pairs of white shorts. Socks and boots were not necessary. The selected players were delighted to pose for a photograph with Peter looking managerial in collar and tie.

When I had called at the Danish project to arrange the football match I had met a tall young man called Hans Telleson. In the course of our conversation I discovered that he enjoyed a game of chess. I had brought my chess set from home and was well practised, having played most days during the lunch break at the pig farm where I had been employed in North Devon.

As I was leaving I said, 'If you feel like a game just come and knock on my door.'

Sure enough, one evening I answered a knock on the door to find that the tall young Dane had taken up my invitation. 'I've come to beat you at chess,' he announced.

I set up the board, got two beers from the fridge and settled down to a three hour battle. I had started playing chess rather late; our children were still attending the small village school where the headmistress was trying to get a chess club going. She invited parents to join. I soon discovered that although I had played a few games in the past, my skills were minimal. A teacher from Barnstaple Grammar School, a keen and accomplished chess player, came along to coach us. I was soon hooked. Our coach gave me a book explaining the openings and defences, which I studied avidly. I discovered that playing against children was good training as they did the most unexpected things. Progress was made. I played second board when we had matches; I joined Barnstaple Chess Club and with a group from this club I played with some twelve others against distinguished visitor Grand Master Golombec. Needless to say he defeated us all. I did feel that I was a half decent performer with a good knowledge of the game.

My first game with Telleson, a worthy opponent, led to regular Thursday evening meetings. One week at his house where we had a meal — invariably chicken as his cook-boy could only prepare this one dish — and the next week at my place where, being my own cook, I attempted to vary the meal within my own limitations. Being evenly matched we had some excellent games and chicken every other week was not so bad.

Telleson had got wind of a chess club outing. We were chatting after one of our Thursday evening contests. It was on a Sunday. Great, I thought; Sundays often found me at a loose end. 'Count me in.'

'They are visiting Munda Wanga Gardens,' said Telleson. 'They are, I understand beautiful gardens and there is a large outdoor chess set, you know where you carry the pieces about.'

I had heard of Munda Wanga but had not yet visited. The reality outdid my expectations. The gardens had been designed by an Englishman and were situated a short drive from Lusaka. There were plants of all descriptions, walks under shady trees, lawns, a swimming pool, refreshment places and a variety of games. The large chess pieces were a central feature of a fine lawn. We didn't try the chess although some others did, but we did some putting, had a game of croquet and performed with credit at table tennis. I was not short of challengers and reflected afterwards that I had played against a polyglot collection of nationalities. There were the usual UK expatriates as well as Danes, Germans, Russians (no sign of the Cold War here) and Israelis, Arabs, East African Asians, both Hindu and Muslim, and two Zambians, all it seemed having a good time together. There was no tension, no religious or political differences, just people enjoying the games and the occasion.

Most would be working on an aid project

of some sort. They would be well qualified in their respective fields, doing worthwhile work. It seemed to me that meeting on neutral territory away from the influences of their native lands, unconcerned about politics or other rivalries, mankind could exist in peace and harmony. Perhaps I take an optimistic view but the sun was shining, the sport had been good, it had been a happy day.

★   ★   ★

Saturday night would often find me at Skottke's for dinner. Skottke had heard that I was a chess player and said he could play chess, we should have a game. I enjoyed our Saturday evening games. They became a regular feature. The Skottkes had television which I didn't have. Lesley would knit and watch television; Skottke would give his full attention to the chess, taking plenty of thinking time before making a move. He defended stoutly but did not have much in the way of an attacking strategy. I was able to enjoy television and play chess at the same time.

10

Health Problems

I was soon to discover that I was expected to be all things to all men and more often than not to all women too. I was awakened one night by an urgent knocking on the door. A group of women, all talking at once, greeted me.

I held up my hands for quiet and one woman stepped forward. 'Bwana we need help. Young girl needs hospital for baby.'

The message was clear enough; I dressed quickly, tossed the mattress from the spare bed and some blankets into the pick-up, got the women aboard and headed for the compound.

The girl in question was young, probably no more than fifteen. The labour pains seemed to be quite frequent. She was screaming with pain and obviously frightened. We made her as comfortable as possible on the mattress. The older women crowded round her, holding her, comforting her, tucking the blankets round her.

'Hurry Bwana, there is not much time,' the

woman who spoke some English said.

I drove furiously to the Lusaka Teaching Hospital. This was the first of several such emergencies.

We were not in a malaria area but I had one case to deal with, probably from an infection picked up elsewhere. It was reported to me that Gotson was talking nonsense and was not well. It was obviously a case for the hospital. Sunday came with me to support Gotson who was not too aware of what was going on. The Russian doctor who examined him said, 'Yes almost certainly he has malaria. Come in a few days.'

When I visited, Gotson was much better. I guessed he had been bathed; he wore clean shorty pyjamas and he was sitting up in a bed with clean sheets. This would have been a new experience for him and a complete contrast to sleeping on a blanket on the hard earth floor of his Nyumba.

An outbreak of whooping cough had me off to the clinic in Chelston for help and advice. I returned with a large container of a soothing linctus. I drove into the compound, peeped my horn and called out, 'All children.' Children began to appear, mothers hustled them into an orderly line. One by one they stepped forward, opened their mouths to accommodate a spoonful of linctus, bobbed their knees and clapped their hands one above the other in the traditional way of expressing thanks. This charming gesture was always observed by children and adults alike for any service rendered. I also included this courtesy in my African vocabulary.

★ ★ ★

The children had long since lost their shyness with me. They tended to play in one large group. One game they invented involved me. They would pick wild flowers and create a garden on the farm road, planting their flowers in rows in the dust. I would happen along in my pick-up. Children would run up the road pointing and shouting. I would pretend not to understand; the children would redouble their efforts to warn me. At the last minute I would stop or swing off into the bush with the cheers and handclapping of the children ringing in my ears. Fortunately this game had a limited lifetime as the children moved on to some other activity.

I was always impressed by the happy faces, the inventiveness and the good manners of the children. They had so little yet there was no delinquency, no vandalism and there was a strong sense of caring for each other. Unfortunately, sometimes a child would die, usually in infancy. My role would be to make a box and perhaps I would be asked to pick up relatives or professional mourners. The sound of keening and wailing would be heard. The box would be borne into the bush where the burial would take place. Someone meantime had brewed some chibuku, made from maize among other things no doubt, and very alcoholic. After the funeral drinking would take place and continue into the night. The next morning would find everything back to normal. Business as usual. That is how death was dealt with.

Peter had received a summons to appear before the Council of Chiefs which performed a function much like our magistrates' courts. His misdemeanour had occurred in a previous employment where Peter had taken it upon himself to burn down a Nyumba which was reputed to have evil spirits within. I heard only a garbled version of this incident but the owner of the Nyumba must have complained to the Chiefs. Peter, having borrowed my pick-up, parked outside the courtroom, went in to face the music and after rigorous questioning, got off with a severe reprimand. When he returned the pick-up to me there was something missing. Someone, in broad daylight, in front of a court of law had removed the spare wheel.

Pay day happened on the Saturday nearest the end of each month. All managers in the corporation had been told not to compete with the commercial farmers. We must pay only the standard wage which was twenty kwachas, equal to ten pounds in U.K. money. I had a large wages book with all the names listed and I entered the amounts due. This I prepared the day before and on wages day I went to the African Bank in Lusaka to collect the exact amount of money. On the afternoon of pay day I set up a table and chair by the implement shed and called the names in turn and counted out the money.

With everybody happy John Tembo would do a trip with the lorry into town for those who wanted to go. Later they would party all night. I never went near the compound on these occasions. Chibuku would be consumed; drums would beat out a rhythm. I could imagine dancing and singing. The drumming and the shouting went on all night; often well into the next morning.

Renee, when she visited, found all this unnerving. She felt threatened by the throb of the drums and the wild carousing. Sometimes a knock on the door next morning would have someone asking for aspirin or a plaster for an injury. Occasionally there would be a more serious injury, probably the result of some dispute. This would mean a trip to Chelston for a proper dressing. Monday morning would see an orderly, sober return to work.

11

A Jinx

Renee was soon to visit; I counted the days and then the hours and was at the airport in good time to meet the plane. As things turned out there seemed to be a jinx on my wife's visits and this was the start of it.

The plane was overdue and then very much overdue. I could get no information except that the plane had trouble in Rome.

'What kind of trouble? Was anyone injured?'

'We don't know, Bwana. Go home, come back later.'

I was extremely worried. The plane was in Rome. There was no information. I went back to the bungalow. The phone was working. I kept calling. I was back at the airport the next morning. Still no news. I waited, then someone on the check-out called me. 'The plane has left Rome. There are no casualties. Everything OK. now, you can come back later.'

The plane landed just after sunset. Renee was fine. She explained. There had been an aborted take off due to smoke coming from a wheel. The chutes had been used to empty the plane quickly. The passengers had been lodged in a hotel overnight. Well, here she was.

I had intended to provide a warm welcome and had asked Lamek to get a fire going for us as a sort of welcome home. When we arrived Lamek was hunkered down beside the fireplace. The room was full of smoke. Not an auspicious start to the holiday. The fire was never lit again.

I thought, to let Renee see some of the sights and so that we could spend time together, I would take some time off and book a trip to the Victoria Falls, just an overnight stay and return the next day. We had opted for a hotel in Livingstone a few miles from the Falls; others, with better local knowledge had booked to stay at the Mosi-oa-Tunja which was hard by the Falls.

All went well for a time; the coach was comfortable, the courier was a pleasant young Zambian girl, there was considerable jollity and much photography through the windows by this collection of different nationalities including a considerable number of Japanese. Then we were all silenced by a loud bang. The bus slowed and lurched over to the side of the road with a burst tyre.

There was a long delay while this was sorted out and we arrived at our hotel as the sun was hurrying down below the horizon. The hotel was of a style left over from colonial days; rooms on all sides of a courtyard, waiters in loose white robes and fez head gear. We were rather tired after a three-hundred-mile trip with a tedious delay and turned in early.

The coach collected us in the morning and we spent the day admiring the Falls, walking along a spray-drenched footbridge dressed in lightweight waterproofs. The Falls are a mile long and a magnificent sight, equally impressive in the dry season when the flow of water is reduced, but the rock formations are interesting; in the wet season it is a thunderous torrent. We kept clear of squatting baboons and resisted the cries of vendors offering half price tourist items. We all assembled for a river boat trip up the Zambezi to view hippos and on this occasion a lone elephant.

'We can't surely have a blow-out this time?' I said as we boarded the coach.

'Don't talk too soon,' Renee replied.

Sure enough, about halfway home there was the now familiar bang. Clued up now, several people said, 'blow out,' as the vehicle pulled over. We were very late home.

I took Renee to Lusaka to look round the two big department stores. Next we called on Ben Van Kuringen at Castcrete. Ben ushered us into his office. 'I'll make some fresh coffee. I have a visitor but don't worry, he's harmless.'

Ben's visitor looked up. Renee gave a little gasp. 'McKenzie!'

The man stared. 'Renee,' he burst out 'the office upstairs.'

'That's right and you were the insurance assessor who came to look at our bashed up vans.'

'Well, well it's a very small world these days,' said McKenzie. 'After we've drunk Ben's coffee and enjoyed his company, follow me home. We can compare notes.'

'And of course this is my husband,' Renee introduced me.

'And what might you be doing out here?' I asked.

'Roads department,' he said. 'I suppose I'm a sort of supervisor.'

Later we followed McKenzie home, which entailed a high speed pursuit, weaving in and out of the traffic, passing on either side, being hooted at, to spend a couple of hours reminiscing and comparing notes.

Back to the bungalow in time for a sundowner, watching the sun disappear, thrilled as always by the wonderful colours.

I had no television, but we had a bottle of wine, plenty of library books, two comfortable chairs and a radiogram. This old fashioned piece of equipment had been supplied by Christie Nel to alleviate my solitary state. It had a radio which seemed only able to find local programmes but the record deck worked; the only snag being that Christie had only been able to supply six records. My favourite was 'Moon River' by Danny Street; then there was 'Sounds Electric', Pat Boon with 'Love Letters in the Sand' . . . the others I can't recall.

There was plenty of insect life on view on the outsides of the window screens, attracted by the light, and no drums to be heard, it was very quiet.

Having done the rounds of visiting friends at various times — a hot curry at Mahdi and Yasmin's, an English meal at the Scottke's, roast lamb at the Nels' — I thought a different outing was overdue.

'How about a trip on the river?' I suggested at breakfast one morning. 'I know a place on the Kafue where we could hire a boat.'

'Are we talking oars or an engine?' she asked.

'Definitely not oars. A small motor launch, probably with an outboard engine. You can loll back on the cushions and trail a languid hand in the water.'

This conversation resulted some two hours later in us heading upriver in a small craft with an outboard motor.

'That conversation we had earlier, you know, about cushions and trailing your hand in the water. I shouldn't — crocodiles. Sorry about the cushions.'

'I'd feel safer on the Thames. Will we see hippos?'

'Yes, but they are safe enough as long as you don't get in among them. If you did they might tip the boat over; but they are vegetarians, they won't eat you.'

'So we get eaten by crocodiles instead.'

'That's about it. That's how the laws of nature work out here, but don't worry, it's a wide river, I will keep well clear of them.'

'I think I would be happier looking at swans on the Thames,' said Renee glumly. We were soon to encounter hippos. As usual they were grouped to one side of the river. We passed hugging the other bank and continued upstream.

I did my best with the birdlife on the banks but was only sure about the fish eagle. I had hoped we might see someone in a dugout canoe but we were out of luck. We had gone perhaps a mile when the engine coughed and gave up. We started to drift downstream on the slow current.

'Just stalled,' I said cheerfully, but the engine stubbornly refused to respond to my pulls on the starter cord. I checked the petrol, plenty in the tank, tickled the carburettor, pulled the cord. A few encouraging coughs but no bursting into life. We drifted.

'We're in midstream, a bit nearer the hippos,' My wife stated what I had increasingly become aware of.

'There's not much we can do about that. We are drifting so slowly, the boat won't steer without the engine. Perhaps we could paddle with our hands?'

Renee pointed to the water. 'Crocodiles.'

'There are not many crocs left. People used to shoot them for sport; in boats with a searchlight, the eyes would reflect the light, bang, one less crocodile. Mindless of course, but young men used to do it.'

'Young men like your friend Nel, I suppose?'

'Yes, Christie used to do it when he was younger; he's moved on to elephants now. I try to get him to mend his ways. He says he only goes hunting once a year, all legal, he buys a licence for two animals, a drop in the ocean he says.'

Conversation palled after this; it was hot in

the sun. We waited. The river seemed to be deserted, nothing moved, our progress was slow but at some point we would encounter the hippos. We debated to and fro, how far? Half a mile, two hundred yards, we had observed no landmarks, we had no idea. Sometimes we thought we heard the beat of an engine but none came our way. Then we were sure we heard something. It was upstream from us and, yes, it was getting louder. It hove into view, another hire boat with a party of holiday makers, all apparently in high spirits. I hailed them. 'We're in trouble, the engine's caput,'

With enormous relief we heard the engine revs drop and the boat came towards us. Alongside they greeted us jovially. 'They must have expected trouble with these boats, there's some rope in this one, we'll tow you back.'

Perhaps four or five hundred yards downstream we passed the hippos peacefully doing what hippos do. Back at base there was much conviviality and we, the rescued, had to submit to being photographed. It was time to leave.

We set off on the trek back to Nkumba. We had missed lunch. It was dark when we reached the bungalow, time for a sundowner and some supper. The Rhodesian boiler would supply plenty of bath water, we could listen to records — choice limited it's true — and enjoy being safe, comfortable and together.

Later Renee said, 'Do you think there's a jinx on me? There was the plane emergency, two burst tyres on the bus trip, then today's engine failure. What do you think?'

I pondered this. 'No jinx, there's no such thing even in Africa. Put it down to happy go lucky maintenance. We call it the Z factor. Next time, could be, nothing will happen.'

Perhaps I spoke too soon.

Renee's holiday was over all too soon. A small group of friends assembled at the airport to see her off. This, I discovered, was the usual courtesy to departing guests.

Skottke turned up, Mahdi and Yasmin were there, the McGees, a Scottish couple we had met, also attended. We sat upstairs drinking coffee till it was time to pass through customs. The others left. I waited and watched the departing plane till it was just a dot in the sky.

★   ★   ★

I had met the McGees quite recently. Stuart McGee had turned up on our doorstep. 'I'm McGee,' he announced, 'I'm a fellow Scot and, like you, a pig farmer.'

We did a tour of the unit then, back indoors, we chatted. I learned that Stuart and Jill McGee came from Marykirk, in Scotland, a place quite obviously close to Stuart's heart. He had retired from the Police Force with the rank of inspector and had turned his attention to pig breeding.

'What brought you to Zambia?' I wanted to know.

'Friends,' he replied. 'I have some friends who are doing market gardening, fields of water melons and the like, not my cup of tea. Pigs are more my line.'

We chatted on for a time and then he left with a pressing invitation for me to visit him soon.

I promised to look him up as soon as I could and so it was that some three weeks later I stood on *his* doorstep. Jill answered my knock. 'Is this a convenient time? Is he about?'

'Nice to meet you, I know who you are,' said Jill offering her hand. 'He's hanging about in the orchard, just over there. He took his flute with him so if you hear something it's not the pipes of Pan.'

I did not hear any music but I did see a music stand and a flute was propped against a tree. Further on I encountered McGee. He was indeed hanging about. Wearing only shorts he hung upside down from a trapeze attached to the stout branch of a tree. His head was about two feet from the ground.

'Nice to see you. I'll get down, not easy to converse upside down.'

'Can you get down?' I asked.

'Piece of cake,' he said and, placing his hands on the ground, he released his legs and was soon the right way up.

I didn't enquire how he got into the position in the first place.

'I suppose you are wondering what I was trying to do.'

'Well yes, I have already learned that you play the flute . . . '

'Rather badly,' he said.

' . . . but I had no idea you were training for a job in the circus.'

McGee smiled ruefully. 'The truth is I have a back problem. Hanging upside down stretches the spinal vertebrae. I think it helps.'

Stuart was quite a character. Wife Jill was keen on horses. Some time later they acquired two riding ponies. One was a leader, the other followed. One day Stuart, not a horse lover, was persuaded to ride out with Jill. He was on the following pony. All went well until the path they were following took a sharp right angle turn. Stuart's mount, following some way behind, decided to take a short cut and leaving the path, took the more direct route through the bush. Anxious to get back in line it quickened its pace. All would have been well if it hadn't decided to duck under a low branch. Stuart could only grab hold and was left wrapped round the branch.

As I heard it, he walked home and could not be persuaded to mount a horse again.

12

An Industrial Dispute

Back at the site things were progressing smoothly, the various teams now well used to their tasks. I set about planning the mill building. It had to be big enough to store part of next year's maize harvest as well as holding bins and milling equipment. The maize would be stored in bulk; walls in the storage area would have to be strengthened and rendered; I had been advised that high tensile wire rolled out along the courses would add to the strength.

I would have steel roof trusses made at an engineering works. It was too big a job for our small workshop. Holding-bins to serve the mill I planned to have made in situ. Again I would go outside for an experienced welder.

Scaffolding was non-existent. So far empty oil drums and planks had sufficed. The mill was high, I would have to think of something. On site we had some gum poles, so useful for termite proof fence posts. Looking at these gave me an idea. I would make two building towers with a solid platform on top. When we fixed the heavy steel roof trusses one tower would be stationed each side to guide the truss into position. The lifting would, like most things in rural Zambia, be done using sheer-legs — three metal poles secured together at the top with the legs spread to form a tripod and a block and tackle to do the work. Of course, with plenty of securely-nailed cross pieces, the towers would also support the bricklayers' planks as the walls rose.

With planning done so far, I collected Sunday and we started marking out. I had no real idea how much space we would need but I decided I would err on the large side anyway. We marked the corners with fence posts and, remembering from school that the diagonals should be equal, we checked and adjusted. With opposite sides equal we thought we had it right. We were at the top of the site but there was still a slight slope; there would be some levelling needed, a job for the tractor grader. The digging gang now had their next target. The bricklayers would be comfortable with it, at least it would be more like a house.

★   ★   ★

Harvest was upon us. Samuel had organised a gang of women and had them in the field, picking cobs. The method was simple enough. The cobs were picked off and put in sacks; the stalks were then bent down to ground level to indicate that the cobs had been harvested. The sacks were collected by tractor and trailer and taken to a sheller. This was effectively a threshing machine which could be towed and sited where needed.

The cobs were fed into the machine which delivered maize to a bagging facility at one end and stover (chaff) to the other. The sacks of maize were stacked on ground liberally sprinkled with insecticide to ward off termites and other creepy crawlies. It was the latter part of June; there would be no rain until November; no need for dryers, tarpaulins, sheds for storage. What a blissful harvest. A considerable amount of stover was bagged and stored for use as bedding in the farrowing houses, the rest would be ploughed in.

But bliss doesn't come easily. We were five days into harvest when the women pickers went on strike. They congregated by the tractor shed, a gesticulating, noisy group, all it seemed talking at once. Their anger seemed to be directed at Samuel who was backing away, adding his voice to the clamour.

He spotted me observing and came over. 'Trouble?' I suggested. Samuel spread his hands. 'Much trouble Bwana, women want more money. More money or no work.'

'Samuel,' I said, 'the Government won't allow me to pay more. There is a rate for the job, that's it.'

I had a lot on my mind, I was exasperated. I gestured towards the women. 'Samuel, just tell them to bugger off.' This was meant only for Samuel's ears but perhaps I had raised my voice a little, I had been heard. Shrieks and arm-waving resulted and one woman broke away to go running off down the road.

'What now Samuel?'

'She goes to police. She says you insulted them.'

'But the police station is eight miles away.'

Samuel said nothing but I could see he was worried. I was worried also. Insulting a Zambian could incur severe penalties. To be declared a prohibited immigrant meant an escorted trip to the airport and a ticket back to your homeland. I had no wish to face this indignity.

Harvest was abandoned for the day and I was left to worry until late in the afternoon. The inevitable Land Rover packed with uniform arrived. I had Samuel by me as a witness and to present my case. He harangued a group of uniformed police with much gesturing and demonstration. The police questioned him at length. I was largely ignored. Then a man emerged from the depths of the Range Rover. He was in plain clothes. When he spoke his English was good.

He came over and shook hands. 'I'm a detective, I trained in U.K. in Birmingham. I will speak to them now.' In English he explained what my 'insult' had amounted to. He concluded, 'In U.K. 'bugger off' is OK. just like 'bullshit', the same, no worse, people say it all the time. Not an insult, just the way they speak in U.K. There is no problem.'

I said, 'I think I have some beer in the fridge, come up to the house. You too Samuel. You should have been a lawyer.' I don't think he fully understood but he looked pleased.

The next day the ladies were back, laughing and chattering, babies slung on their backs. It was as if nothing had happened.

Harvest was more or less taking care of itself; the area of trodden-down stalks was growing and a mini mountain of sacks in the centre of the field was testament to a good yielding crop.

* * *

Our children would be out to spend some of their school holiday with me. I was looking forward to that and thinking of ways to keep them occupied. I had always enjoyed a game of table tennis — so, why not. I ordered the necessary size of chipboard, had John Tembo collect it on his next trip to town and set about painting it green with a white edging to it.

The previous occupant had left a large dining table and chairs; the table tennis top sat nicely on the table and there it stayed for the period of my contract. Once I had purchased the net and the bats I was ready to try it out. Mahdi had shown an interest in all this and indeed had helped with the painting. He was already established as a left hand spin bowler in a Muslim cricket team but had not become involved with the football.

I asked him, 'Do you play table tennis?'

'I have played — a bit,' he replied.

'We could play some day in our spare time,' I suggested.

He agreed, and we did. I soon discovered he had played — a bit. More than a bit, he played like a champion. He could beat me easily with his less good right hand, and, although I never beat him, my game improved. The table tennis proved to be a big hit with visitors. Skottke liked a game. Rather like his chess game he was very defensive, He concentrated on returning every ball and was a difficult man to get a winner past.

* * *

The workshop was producing water tanks, securely welded and painted inside with epoxy tar, the outside with grey undercoat and gloss. To support these some building work was required at the end of each house. I felt strongly that header tanks were essential as insurance against an interruption in the water supply.

I also felt that toilets were needed. It was not always easy to know when someone was missing. I would ask, 'Where is Cobra?' and the reply, 'He is in the bush Bwana,' was not very helpful. Too many people were visiting too often. With enough toilets on site no one would need to visit the bush. Now was my chance to provide toilets with little or no extra work.

The stands for the tanks would be hollow rectangles built over the slurry drain. There would be an entrance, a concrete floor with a hole in it and a water supply with a short length of hose for washing down after use. When enough had been built I would make it a rule that no one should leave the site without permission.

I had hoped we would have one side of the development done by the end of my first full year, i.e. 1971. I also wanted to see the mill building well on its way. We were on target for this and it was time to start getting water into the buildings and also finish off the slurry channels by fitting baffles.

Plumbing was fairly straight forward, using polythene pipe and brass conex fittings. Each pen would have a 'stingy' drinker fitted in the dunging passage. The slurry channels required a concrete block at intervals on the floor with a downward baffle held in channel iron on either side, two inches off the block and two inches lower than the top of the block. The slurry, responding to the pull of gravity would rise over the block and escape through the narrow aperture causing turbulence.

This simple system, requiring no mechanical power, would convey slurry to either side of the site to discharge into exactly similar drains which would empty into large pits, dug into the ground, lined with rendered blockwork to be pumped on to the land. The side drains which picked up the laterals from the houses down the line to the holding pits did not need to be any larger, all that happened was that the rate of flow increased.

The fattening houses now had gates fitted in the dung passages and farrowing crates for the farrowing houses had been programmed. The workshop was busy.

101

Harvest was progressing without the time and weather pressures that I had been used to. Indeed it would soon be over. Maize from outlying fields was being carted to the existing stack where it would eventually be transported to the Government storage in Lusaka. Protected against termites and other pests by a liberal ground dressing of insecticide and with no rain until November there was no great pressure to move it until the harvest was completed.

It was on one of these harvest days in July when Mahdi pulled up in haste at my front door. I knew right away that something was wrong when he failed to observe the usual courtesies, a knock on the door, a shouted 'Odi', the African equivalent of 'Anybody home?' Instead he pushed the door open and stood inside obviously disturbed about something. I waited for an explanation.

'It's Peter,' he said, 'his car is in the side of the road about ten miles back. He is flat out, could be dead, head hanging over the back of the seat.'

'You didn't stop?'

'I thought he might have been robbed. Bandits could have been hanging about in the bush. I came for help.' Mahdi waited, obviously looking to me to provide a plan of action. I went to my bedroom and collected my single-barrelled shotgun and a handful of cartridges.

'We'll pick up the watchman from the site,' I suggested. It was afternoon and the site was guarded from the time the work stopped at two.

We drove to the building site and recruited the watchman. He carried a spear; not, I noted of traditional construction; it was a short length of mild steel rod flattened and sharpened at one end. I recognised this as a product of the farm workshop.

Ten miles back along the dirt road we came on Peter's car, a Citroen C3, well down over the steep camber of the road, but pulled up short of the bush beyond. Peter, motionless, head lolling backwards was in the driver's seat. If this was the work of bandits, they could easily be concealed in the dense bush beyond the car.

The watchman stood up and adopted a warlike stance; Mahdi pointed the gun to cover my approach to the car. I hoped that in any ensuing melee I would not be peppered by my own gun. I approached the car with some misgivings; there was a corpse-like quality about young Peter but as soon as I opened the car door the mystery was solved.

The normally abstemious Peter was well and truly drunk.

Struggling with the strange gears of the C3, I drove Peter home to sleep it off.

The next day being Sunday, Peter had no reason to surface early. I encountered him in the afternoon. He could recall attending a rugby match in Lusaka and having been invited to have a drink in the clubhouse afterwards. I was to learn that his tolerance to alcohol was extremely low.

This particular Sunday would end like every other day — with a glorious sunset. At 6am the next day work would resume on the farm and on the building site. The workshop would be busy making farrowing crates, gates, tanks and maybe, just maybe, the odd surreptitious spear.

13

School Holidays

I was at the airport waiting to greet my children. The plane had landed and people were trickling through. I waited. Lots of people came through, no sign of them yet, I was getting anxious. Then a girl appeared. Blonde streaks in her hair, smartly dressed with short skirt, it took me a moment or two to register that this was Patricia, our daughter, all grown up. There was a short delay and then John appeared. He hadn't changed much: the same long hair, the grubby parka, the flared jeans; I guessed he had been stopped for questioning. Patricia (we always called her Trish) saw me and waved. I left the waiting area and nipped in to help them through the formalities. Nobody stopped me and we were soon upstairs having a bite to eat. Then the journey to the farm with much to talk about.

The first day they were down on the site. John became the official pick-up driver, moving supplies as required, Trish his co-pilot. They seemed happy enough doing this, playing table tennis in the afternoon or braving the cold, deep, well water of the reservoir for a swim.

Soon they were part of the team, well accepted by all except, in John's case, the smaller children, who cried and hid their faces every time he confronted them. I think they had never seen a man with long hair.

However I thought it was not enough to be around the site or driving in the bush in the afternoons. I felt they really must see the Victoria Falls. Skottke offered to change vehicles over a weekend. I jumped at the offer. A three hundred mile journey in the pick-up did not appeal and the offer of a real car was heaven sent. We packed up some food and drink and set off. The road was a narrow ribbon of tarmac with gravel either side, steeply sloping. We met the occasional car and partly pulled off the tarmac, the approaching car taking an equal share of the tarmac and the gravel. With little traffic and miles of straight road we made good progress, stopping only once to picnic in the shade of some roadside trees.

Eventually, rather weary, we parked outside the Mosi-oa-Tunja hotel.

'I'll just pop in and book our accommodation.' I said.

Of course I had not booked ahead. I could

not believe that all the rooms would be taken — but they were; we could have dinner and breakfast in the morning but would have to sleep elsewhere. My companions took it well.

John said, 'Mum would have booked ahead.'

Trish said, 'We can sleep in the car Dad. It will be more of an adventure.'

'Bags the back seat,' said John.

And so, after seeing the sights and snapping photos, we parked the car among some trees near the falls, watched the setting sun and settled down to survive the night. John arranged his length as best he could on the back seat. Trish and I reclined our seats as far as possible and we all tried to sleep. This did not come easily and we were aware as the night progressed that the cold increased. Wearing lightweight day clothes and with not even a rug in the car, by sunrise we were somewhat chilled, rather cramped and uncomfortable.

Trish suggested a run. She and I set off along a path by the river and ran until warmth returned to our bodies. John opted for a bit more fitful sleep. We then set off in the car, the heater on high, warm and relaxed to explore the track alongside the Zambezi. We were enjoying the ride and in high spirits until we rounded a corner and nearly ran into a large elephant. I stood on the brakes and

107

fumbled for reverse gear.

We were so close we seemed to be looking up its trunk. It wasn't apparently too pleased about meeting us either. It raised its head, curled its trunk upwards and gave us an ear-splitting warning. By this time reverse gear was engaged and we were moving backwards at speed. Out of sight round the corner I turned the car round and set off the way we had come.

'Well, that was an adventure,' I said trying to sound jovial.

'Can we have some breakfast now?' said John, obviously having had enough adventure for one day.

Back at the hotel we washed and brushed up in the toilets and had a very hearty breakfast. Thus fortified, we visited a small game park nearby, scratched a recumbent cheetah behind the ears through some wire mesh and were rewarded by some happy purring. On the way to the exit a tame zebra accosted us looking for titbits. We didn't even have a biscuit for it.

We had an early lunch and set off for Nkumba. On the drive back I asked John what he thought of it so far. 'Eventful,' he said after a moment's thought.

And that probably just about summed it up.

Table tennis proved to be a great success. It had not featured much in their lives up to now and they practised assiduously. Their ambition was to beat me. Of course with the stretching of my game playing against the invincible Mahdi I had improved enough to appear to be unbeatable to the children. They would warm up against each other then one or the other of them would challenge me. I would let my challenger get a few points ahead only to draw level at twenty. Excitement levels would rise as we battled for a winner. I would try to win by landing one on the very edge of the table and be accused of winning by a lucky shot.

And so we compensated for no television, no real music deck, no telephone calls to friends. This and reading filled their evenings. Both read 'The Tontine,' a nine hundred page tome, among others of my library books collected by the armful about every two weeks.

I was surprised at how little they seemed to miss the trappings of a more sophisticated world.

★ ★ ★

It was Ben Van Kuringen's idea that we should visit the Kariba Dam.

'The kids should see it. It's a great piece of engineering and I have a friend down there who has a boat. We will be able to see the dam from the lake.'

One Sunday we drove down in Ben's V.W. Combi. On the way we stopped to explore a wonderful petrified forest. This was something we might never see again, a forest turned to stone, exposed by wind erosion after being buried for centuries.

Ben's friend had a boat hire business which appeared to involve dropping groups of people — families, friends, at various favoured coves and beaches round the lake where they could picnic, swim, fish or laze in the shade. Our boat trip was the afternoon pick up which allowed us to see a lot of the lake and we had a good viewing of the dam.

Although the power station was on the Rhodesian (as it was called then) side of the dam, Kariba also supplied Zambia.

As the visit neared its end I decided to take John and Trish out to dinner. The hotel was one I had not visited; it seemed to fit the bill. We had to dress up a bit; John had put aside his flares in favour of smart trousers and shirt. Trish of course was dolled up with a bit of make-up on as a final touch and I was in long trousers, shirt and cravat. The head waiter greeted us, elegant, dinner-suited, an imposing figure. I explained we hadn't booked but would like a table for dinner. He looked us over and pointed to John. 'No tie, bare arms, it is not good, I cannot let you have a table.'

I looked around the diners. 'Plenty of short sleeve safari suits,' I pointed out.

This didn't impress him. 'No tie,' he said, 'you must leave.'

I had driven twenty miles. This was supposed to be a treat for my offspring. 'We are not going anywhere. We will stand here until you find us a table. Unless of course you intend to throw us out. Then we will make a fuss.'

'Please Bwana, no fuss, just leave.'

I did not reply but stood my ground in full view of the diners, arms folded.

He sighed and left us. We waited. When he returned he said. 'Follow me, I give you a table.'

Our table was tucked away behind a pillar. He seated us, sighed again and said rather wearily, 'Enjoy your meal.'

With the tension removed and, apart from the siting of the table, victory achieved, we laughed and joked our way through an excellent meal.

All too soon the holiday was over. At the airport Trish sailed up the escalator waving and smiling. John was stopped by two security men and questioned before being allowed to pass. I could see the worry on his face and felt for him, but a grubby parka, long hair and flared trousers with coloured inserts almost invited interrogation.

With the family gone I felt a bit bereft but I planned to take my leave in October or perhaps November. Mahdi would plant the maize in my absence if my leave went into November. Ploughing was in full swing. Mahdi had the huge disc ploughs weighed down with bags of stones. Deep ploughing was a must; forty acres of sunflowers was also planned. Mahdi was fully briefed on this. We were to use Russian seed and a Russian adviser had been active in Zambia promoting the crop and advising on its management. I had selected forty acres right in front of my bungalow for this project and looked forward to a colourful display.

On the site I hoped that in my first full year, two fattening houses and two farrowing houses would be complete, including all slurry drains, plumbing for drinkers, as well as a metal pipe through the middle of each house with quick release fittings at intervals for use with a hose pipe for washing down.

Header tanks for each house would also be necessary.

I had in mind to swill down twice a day. Clean houses would be less attractive to flies and the pigs would love a cooling shower twice a day. The washing-down water would be pumped from the borehole pump directly into the metal pipe network. A release valve, suitably set at the end of the line would ensure that nothing became over pressurised.

So far we were on course but if we did finish one side and perhaps start on the second phase there was still much to be done. I hoped the mill would be well on its way when I went on leave. So, for the second year we had to achieve a mirror image of the first year which still left a service building for weaned sows and boars, dry sow accommodation and gilt housing. There was also some serious digging to be done to build holding wells for the slurry. All this would be complicated by the introduction of stock in the second half of the year.

I had been in touch with an engineer who would make and supply the steel roof trusses for the mill. He arranged to come out and have a look. He measured up, made notes, did his calculations, gave me a price and said, 'No problem. Build the trusses into the last two courses of block-work, slope one way to the back, delivery in about six weeks. There will be lugs to take timber purlins to suit your sheeting.'

All very satisfactory, all very easy. I could see the roof being on soon after my leave. I wanted to be present when this took place. Health and safety was ever present in my mind, not something that bothered my nimble, barefooted work force.

★ ★ ★

Working on the principle that all work and no play is not the best way to foster team spirit I contacted my Danish friends about a date for our long-awaited football fixture. Yes, they now had a team, yes, they would play at Nkumba. We arranged a date, our team put in some serious practice, confidence was high, and the excitement was evident.

Match day was upon us. The visiting team did not arrive in a lorry or farm tractor; they came like a real football team in a large, rather fine bus. One thing we had overlooked was the appointment of a referee. It had been assumed by all that I would do this. Peter was in the team, Mahdi was a non-footballer with no knowledge of the game. Reluctantly I took the whistle. I had not wanted to arbitrate in the heated atmosphere of a football match.

Half time arrived with no goals scored. I thrust the whistle at a Danish spectator and was free to support my team. We had a consultation; I suggested that the most likely source of goals would be from crosses into the box. Sunday was good with his head and Peter had a powerful shot. The goals duly came as the opposition tired; Sunday nodded in two and Peter nicked one in the dying minutes.

The game had attracted quite a few spectators. Most of the compound population had turned out and some had come on the bus from the Danish project. The celebrations were long and exuberant. The football team was launched and with a win.

I set about arranging a fixture list for our young team and their fans to look forward to. Of necessity most games would be played away as, unlike the Danish project, not everyone had a bus or even a lorry.

14

Home Leave

The time had come for me to pass on my worries and responsibilities. I was off on leave. It was on this leave home that Renee decided to come back with me and give it a go. Arrangements had to be made for John and Patricia. We found a landlady in Barnstaple who would take them and look after them. Whatever we did it was not going to be easy to leave them behind. Then there was the dog; Meg, the last of my sheepdogs, was fourteen years old. I had her checked over; could she tolerate an eleven hour flight? The vet thought she would be all right, a bit of arthritis, eyes not too good, hearing likewise, but she should be alright. He gave me some tranquillisers to ease her anxiety and finally said, 'Get her immunised against rabies when you get there.'

A travelling box was the next requirement. This I ordered from Spratts, to be delivered at Heathrow in time for our flight. With the house let for six months and my leave over we seemed to be all set; all that remained was to see our son and daughter settled in and say our goodbyes. This was the hard part; John was doing his best to be stoical, Trish was in floods of tears. Renee and I were trying to present a stiff upper lip, and then we were being driven to the station by a friend and we were on our way.

Our flight was not the usual stop at Rome, down through Italy, across the Sahara. This time we were to stop at Cyprus. However the jinx seemed to be with us and we circled Cyprus for an age before the captain announced a change of plan. Due to turbulence we were unable to land and were going on to Beirut. We duly landed in the middle of the night and with few facilities open we spent a miserable two hours, alleviated only by strong coffee. We were concerned that the long delays would be affecting Meg, kennelled in the hold. We explained our concerns to a stewardess who arranged for a forklift to take us out to have a look. The forklift driver opened a door and hoisted us up. Meg's box was just inside; she was sleepy but pleased to see us in a tired sort of way. I made sure she had plenty of water and, somewhat relieved, we settled down to await our tardy departure.

At last our long journey was over. Meg was delivered to us; Mahdi was there to drive us to the sanctuary of our bungalow. We rested up most of the day. Meg had travelled really well. She sorted out a rug to sleep on and didn't seem unhappy to rest the day away.

In late afternoon Mahdi came in to report. The rains had been good so far.

About seven hundred acres had been planted after pre-emergence weed killer had been applied. This included the forty acres of sunflowers. No problems in this department. On the building site work had progressed, with only a few odds and ends to clear up on the first four buildings. Work on the mill building could go ahead now.

I felt that some site tidying was in order. One area would not have any more traffic on it; I thought that some ploughing and levelling was in order with a view to establishing some grass. My information was that Kikuyu grass was the answer. This grass would spread by pushing out above-ground shoots, (stolons) and would survive the long dry period.

I was directed towards the Lusaka racecourse where the grass was used. Here I met a lady who was in charge of all things pertaining to the racecourse and the racing and as an extra, ran the Lusaka Agricultural Show. Quite a remarkable woman. At first she was a little reluctant to have me dig up her grass but eventually found an unused corner where I might collect some stolons.

These were planted in well worked soil and soon spread to give us a green area to rest our eyes on. To me this operation seemed all wrong; like planting a field back home with couch grass, a persistent weed grass which spread by underground shoots (rhizomes) and was difficult to eradicate; however this tough drought resistant plant was the answer to a dry climate. I was pleased with the result when we eventually had the makings of a lawn. Now we needed a lawn mower and a man to work it.

John Tembo collected a mower and I had someone in mind to look after the grass and general tidiness. John Mombasa, one of the older workers was having trouble with his eyes. He would be less at risk cutting grass, painting water tanks and other lighter jobs. John had no English except, 'yes Bwana'. When I suggested his new role his reply was predictable.

The mill building was up to height. The heavy steel trusses had to be hoisted into position. I had plenty of men on the job. Some armed with long poles to stop the trusses swinging out of control. A tower with two men aboard was stationed at either side to guide the truss into its resting place. A team at ground level worked the block and tackle and hoisting began. The men with the poles took care of any tendency to swing about as the truss was slowly raised and guided into its resting place.

The job was much easier than I had expected. The roof trusses were blocked in and the next day the roof timbers were fitted, once again using the building towers. Once it was sheeted in I heaved a sigh of relief. There had been no mishaps. We had a safe haven for the milling machinery when it arrived.

★ ★ ★

There appeared to be no game around Nkumba except for the tiny dik-dik, a miniature of the antelope breed. There were of course, wild pigs, monkeys, and guinea fowl and on one occasion I saw an ant bear in my headlights crossing the farm road as it pursued its nocturnal foraging. There must have been warthogs around at one time because Christie Nel told me of a pet warthog that he had rescued as a baby and which as an adult used to run with his four dogs behind his Land Rover as he went about his farm. Unfortunately a rabid dog had visited one day. The dogs and the warthog had been involved in an attack. Christie had shot the offending dog and sadly had no option but to shoot his dogs and Warty the warthog.

In his young days Christie had a pet dik-dik, also rescued and hand reared which lived out its life on the farm. This was another side of Christie the hunter who shot elephants, lions and a variety of antelopes for trophies and the thrill of the hunt. He sometimes popped over to see how I was spending my leisure time and one day he took me for a bush ride in his Land Rover. We followed paths and obscure tracks or drove directly through the bush, knocking over saplings and forcing a path through thickets. We were both taken by surprise when, emerging from thick bush into a clearing we saw before us a female Kudu with a well grown calf by her side. They took off with Christie in pursuit. He reached for the rifle he always carried behind his seat. Bumping along at considerable speed he held the rifle one handed outside the window and fired off a shot. The adult Kudu continued her flight, the calf dropped in its tracks. We pulled up, Christie leapt out, the calf was still alive, the bullet had grazed its head, it was starting to come round. Christie whipped out a sheath knife from his belt and expertly cut its throat.

I could see the excitement, the tension in

him. This was the hunter. This was his legitimate game. Food for the family.

'One for the deep freeze. I'll skin it, do the butchery job and bring some over.'

I looked at the flies already swarming on the spill of blood. This was sudden violent death. Not like sending farm animals to an abattoir for humane slaughter. Somehow this was different — but was it? It was as if I had witnessed an unnecessary killing, violent and unprovoked and Christie had enjoyed it.

I felt queasy. 'You keep it, it's yours.' Nevertheless Christie did bring a joint over. We cooked it and ate it. It was delicious.

★ ★ ★

Now settled in, Renee set about job hunting. With Lamek doing everything except the cooking she needed an occupation. The novelty of sleeping-in a little and having tea served in bed by Lamek began to pall. Very soon she was in touch with a well known firm of accountants with offices in Lusaka who were keen to employ her. However with everything agreed the Z factor kicked in. Renee had been working in accountancy for years. A combination of a long apprenticeship, hard work and some home study was at that time good enough for U.K. employers. It was also good enough for the company in Lusaka which wanted to engage her, it was not good enough for the Zambian Government. In the eyes of the Government she was unqualified. There was a rule that required all expatriates who wished to work in Zambia to have formal qualifications. Renee did not have the required qualifications. She was not allowed to work in Zambia.

This was a bitter pill to swallow but, resourceful to the end Renee decided to create a voluntary job. She would try to teach the English language to Losta, Lamek's older girl. It was a matter of sadness to both Renee and I that Losta, in common with all but two of the children on the farm had little hope of an education. The two exceptions were Peter's children. Every morning just after six Peter would set off on his motor bike — the two children mounted behind — to attend school in Chelston. The school operated on a shift system, morning children and afternoon children.

Losta was just a year younger than our Trish. On each of her holiday visits Renee would bring with her some of Trish's outgrown clothes for Losta who now had a better than average wardrobe. Now Renee hoped to improve her lot by teaching her some basic English. Not many women on the farm could speak more than a few words of English. The men for the most part could speak and understand some English having more contact with it in their employment.

Lamek was of course delighted with the arrangement. Losta would come to the house on two afternoons a week. Lessons started, but it was uphill work. Unlike children in more sophisticated societies Losta had not grown up with trains, buses, aeroplanes or even cats, cows, horses or animals in a zoo. She had never been to a town or seen a lion, even in a picture book. However Renee persevered with objects with which Losta was familiar, table, chair, rug, door and food, maize, potatoes, yams, sunflowers, mangoes, avocado and so on. It brought home to us that children in developed countries would have absorbed a lot of images and that many things were familiar to them when they started school. However Renee soldiered on, trying to overcome Losta's difficulties, encourage Lamek to make a contribution and was able to report a little progress.

Losta was a pretty girl but what did the future hold for her? Perhaps in a year or so some young man would come along, offer Lamek some money and bear Losta off to share his Nyumba. Soon she would have children of her own. We hoped that she might have a year or two of her childhood left before sliding into womanhood and child bearing.

Meg our elderly sheepdog had had a new lease of life. The climate did nothing for her failing sight or reduced hearing, but the arthritis which had stiffened her limbs in U.K. responded well to the warm sunshine. She spent her days either with me on the site or walking with Renee. On the site she would find a cool place to sleep or if the pick-up was parked in the shade she would be happy on the bench seat with the windows open. She became very possessive about the pick-up. If someone approached and looked in the window she would curl her lip and snarl. On the other hand if Sunday walked up opened the door and got in she took no notice.

★　★　★

Our first full year was on target both in terms of budget and progress. Skottke had not heard that the budget had been approved at Government level but it seemed that Mr Kapota was aware and happy with our efforts. L.P.O.s were being processed and paid, in fact Skottke had heard whispers that Mr Kululu the Minister for Rural Development would like to pay us an official visit.

'Not before the feed mill is operational,' I

said. 'Hold them off for bit.'

Skottke said he would do his best.

I planned to get a service building and some dry sow accommodation built before I introduced pigs. We could then get half the unit working. By then I hoped we would be producing our own rations. I heard no more about the official visit and rather dismissed it from my mind. The milling machinery arrived. It was simple enough to assemble; a Hammer Mill securely fixed, trunking to convey ingredients from the bins to the mill, and gearing to adjust amounts from each bin. I now needed an electrician to make it all work. Our experienced welder was now needed to build the bins to suit the job. This was not an easy task with bin panels cut to shape and hoisted by block and tackle to be spot welded initially, but many hands do make the work easier and eventually we had a working feed mill.

* * *

One of Skottke's duties was to accompany Mr Kamanga the Minister for Agriculture on various farm visits. His role was that of advisor. With a considerable workload, I knew he found this inconvenient. I had a very early phone call on one occasion. 'I'm not too good this morning. Could you do me a favour?'

'Yes,' I answered cautiously, 'but it depends on the favour.'

'Well today I was to accompany Mr Kamanga on some visits. One, a pig farm owned by a Government Minister. I really don't feel up to it. I thought you might take my place.'

'Not keen,' I said. 'Are you sure you're not up to it?'

'I feel rotten. I'm still in bed I don't think I could cope with it today.'

'All right,' I agreed reluctantly, 'what do I do?'

'Report to the Department of Agriculture at 8am. There will be some black limos lined up. Go inside and report. Make my excuses. Park behind the black cars.'

'Right,' I said, 'I think I can cope with that part of it. What else?'

'At the farm, stand next to Mr Kamanga, he may need some help. Keep the questions going. You'll soon get the hang of it.'

'Okay,' I said, 'wish me luck. Get well soon.'

I mentally cancelled my plans for the day and thought perhaps I had better smarten up a little. Shorts and sandals would hardly be acceptable. I went to my wardrobe. My safari suit hung, washed and pressed. Below, my brown shoes, well polished, waited.

Lined up behind three smartly chauffeured cars and having reported to a desk inside, I waited for the off. Mr Kamanga emerged with members of his staff and filled the cars in front. I hoped that he had received my message that Skottke was laid low. And then we were off. I soon realised that my Toyota pick-up was going to be hard put to it to keep up. I drove flat out in the dust trail of the limos.

At last we reached our first visit, the pig farm. I ranged myself up beside the Minister.

'Sorry Skottke is unwell. What is the trouble?'

'Sounded like a sore throat, he was a bit hoarse.'

'Ah well, you are the pig expert aren't you. I am not knowledgeable about pigs. You will know what to say.'

Our host greeted us and the tour began. As we stopped at intervals to talk about points of interest I felt that my advisory task was upon me. I asked questions along the lines of . . . 'I am sure the Minister would like to know . . . ' This tactic was quite successful. I asked the question, the answer was given to Mr Kamanga.

Our next visit was to a research station where, among other things they were breeding strains of grass which were drought resistant. I found this very interesting and continued my method of supporting the Minister. There was tea, after which I asked Mr Kamanga if he would excuse me as I had pressing business back at Nkumba.

I drove back at my own pace, glad not to be following in someone's dust cloud. Since I had to pass near Blue Boar Road, I decided to look in on the ailing Skottke. Lesley and their large dog greeted me.

'How's the invalid?' I asked. 'Ah,' said Lesley. 'He's somewhere in the Eastern Province at the moment. He felt so much better.'

Wonderful powers of recovery? Or was it tactics? I didn't care either way. I'd had an interesting day and had managed the diplomacy well enough. Still I didn't want to make a habit of it.

15

The Official Visit

Renee and I were spending a Sunday morning cruising in the pick-up travelling roads we did not often use. We found ourselves on a good dirt road, wide, well surfaced, steeply cambered; I slowed as we reached a bend. On the bend a bridge carried us over a stream cut deeply between two banks. Just round the bend we were flagged down by an excited group of people. We pulled up. Someone shouted, 'Accident Bwana,' and pointed. We looked down at the stream, some ten feet below the road. A smart red sports car, badly damaged, had obviously left the road, plunged down to the stream and hit a tree, bonnet first. There was no one in the car, a coupé with the hood down. We turned our attention to the people grouped by the side of the road. In their midst a woman cradled a young girl perhaps eight years old. She was bloodstained and unconscious. A fast drive to hospital was indicated. Standing apart was an older girl — we learned later that she was seventeen years old

— who seemed to have escaped injury, wailing and crying and could not be comforted.

The injured girl, still deeply unconscious, we made as comfortable as possible on Renee's lap; I didn't give much for her chances. The older girl had to go in the back where she stood holding on and still hysterical. I was not happy with this arrangement, would she hold on? She refused to sit — but I had to get the young girl to hospital. I prayed we would not have another accident. I drove fast, time was of the essence. We rushed into the hospital Renee still cradling the injured girl, the older girl following, still shouting. Hospital staff took over; the young girl was quickly despatched, presumably to a cubicle for examination or straight to an operating theatre. We were no longer in the picture and we waited some time before we had any information. The older girl was taken to a ward. Renee was asked if she would mind sitting with her. I sat in a corridor waiting for news. Later when we compared notes. Renee described the ward where she comforted the elder girl. A mix of ages, both sexes, a confusion of ailments. While she sat there, with the girl settling down to quiet sobbing, a man got up from a nearby bed. He had obviously been badly burned; shreds of loose skin festooned his body, he was completely naked and a nasty discharge from his penis was obviously troubling him as he shambled past heading for a toilet.

The girls' parents arrived, distraught, inconsolable. They were taken in hand by staff. Some two hours later we heard that the young girl had died. Renee reported that the older girl had calmed a little and thought maybe she had been sedated.

We drove to the Skottke's house in Blue Boar Road just outside Lusaka. Renee, was able to get out of her bloodstained clothes, get cleaned up, borrow some clean clothes and have a strong cup of tea.

Later we heard the whole sad story. The father owned a garage in Lusaka. He had given his daughter the sports car for her seventeenth birthday. She had taken her young sister out for a spin with the tragic result in which we had played a part.

I could well imagine the course of events. The joy of the elder girl, a happy moment the younger girl wanted to share; the exuberance of their spirits as they set off for their spin. The corner looming, the speed too fast, the road surface firm but with a coating of loose latherite gravel, the tyres not gripping, the terror as the car flew into the void. All over in seconds.

A further sad footnote. We heard that the parents could not forgive or be reconciled with the surviving girl and at some point she left home.

The harvest had started when we were given a date for the official visit. Preparations were afoot. Approach roads and site roads were being graded. Our grass area was being cut; it was now a passable lawn. Odds and ends of building material were being tidied up. Workers were briefed to keep working on the day, not to stop and stare.

The mill was swept. Maize was being stored. There was now a stout wall across the mill building which created a bulk storage area occupying a third of the floor space. Into this wall we had built in an empty oil drum with both ends removed; this provided a low level extraction point where an auger could be introduced.

I proposed that we should meet and have the speeches in the mill after which I would demonstrate the workings of the mill. I did not intend to have a full milling session, just a demonstration of moving grain, with the mill running empty, making sure in advance that it was free from dust. One auger would transfer grain from the store to a bin which would be discharging into a container, to be conveyed back to the store by another auger. Our mill had not yet achieved the final objective. We had a bin part way down the unit into which I proposed to blow the mixed meal but this operation was held up awaiting the right size of piping. Meantime the meal was blown through a bottomless sack to make a heap on the floor. Not really for the eyes of officialdom. The boisterous hum of the empty hammer mill and the clatter of the augers, I hoped might impress the visitors.

The workshop would be another point of interest. I planned to have people cutting and drilling component parts with a gate being welded and some we had made earlier on show. The slurry drainage system would be explained and a tour of the buildings would be on the cards. I made sure that Skottke would explain that all this wonderful work was done by unskilled workers trained at Nkumba.

We now had two fattening houses, two farrowing houses, a service house and a dry sow house well on the way. The slurry system for this side of the development was complete except for the large storage wells yet to be dug. Groundwork had started on the mirror image; pigs would soon have to feature.

★   ★   ★

The great day arrived. Skottke was with me to greet the dignitaries. We waited. A dust cloud heralded the approach of the Government cars on the dirt road. Soon they swept into the unit, six large black limousines, chauffeur driven, flags flying, to park in a neat line by the mill. Mr Kululu had obviously brought a large section of his department with him.

Skottke stepped forward to meet the minister and to introduce me. Mr Kululu, a small, courteous man shook hands and said. 'I am impressed by what I see, I think today we can declare Nkumba officially opened. We can assemble in this fine building; perhaps you or Mr Skottke can welcome us.' He raised an eyebrow.

'I am sure Mr Skottke has planned to do that,' I said hurriedly.

Mr Kululu nodded and went on, 'then I shall make a speech and declare the project open. Perhaps then you could show us round.'

Skottke opened proceedings with a speech of welcome and explained in a few words the aims of the project. Mr Kululu spoke next and declared Nkumba officially opened. A digging gang should have been busily working on the second phase foundations. It would appear that work had stopped; this was obviously to be a spectator occasion. A tour of the buildings followed. I did my best to explain the slurry system. I had Sunday standing by with a drum of water for the demonstration. I introduced him as the site foreman; he tipped the water in and we all watched the turbulence as the water rapidly disappeared along the drain. In the farrowing house I explained the farrowing crates which could quickly convert to loose housing and informed the Minister that pigs would soon feature.

Back in the mill I explained the grain storage and how the maize would be moved. I pressed a switch and an auger sprang into life. I then engaged the other auger and set the hammer mill going. This was greeted by a burst of hand clapping and some cheering. Things were going well.

★   ★   ★

A few days later Skottke was able to tell me that the budget had been approved.

With the thought of pig farming about to start in earnest I was keen to get a complete unit working. There was still some work to be done, the dry sow house was not finished but more importantly there was a need to get the large slurry storage pits, at least the ones on the first phase, dug, lined and plastered. I was unwilling to deplete the gang preparing footings on the second phase so I decided we needed to recruit more workers. Apart from anything else, some site workers would have to transfer to pig work. This would entail some training in the foreseeable future.

With all this in mind I decided to visit a shanty town on the fringes of Lusaka where there would be many unemployed. Rather reluctantly Renee agreed to come with me.

'Might as well see the worst side of Lusaka,' she said.

The reality was probably worse than she had imagined. We drove into the centre of a collection of homes that beggared belief. All huddled close together, shacks made from the throw away residues of more prosperous parts of the town. Bits of wood, cardboard, rusty corrugated iron, metal drums that had been cut open and flattened.

As we pulled up a child went into a latrine, a structure made from elephant grass supported by a few stakes and string. Urine seeped under the grass surround and made a rivulet in the dust. We did not have time to dwell on such things. In minutes we were surrounded by young men.

'Do you want workers Bwana?' someone shouted.

'I want six men for building work,' I said.

There was much jostling as everyone tried to push to the front. It was incumbent on me to choose the fittest. The work they would be doing was physically hard. I picked my first young man. 'Get what you want from your house and come back.' I repeated this exercise five more times. I could see the disappointment in the eyes of those not favoured. I picked two more but had to the draw the line somewhere. The pick-up would be overloaded as it was.

Realising that there were no more jobs on offer, the crowd dispersed. Soon the successful ones returned, laughing and joking. Nobody had asked any questions. They had no idea where I was taking them. They were not going to lose the chance of a job by asking questions. This was the extent of the unemployment situation in and around Lusaka at that time.

We drove out of the shanty town with mixed feelings; glad to be in the open countryside again but saddened by what we had left behind; a place, overcrowded, unsanitary, no doubt with high infant mortality and disease. It had been a sobering experience. Renee was very quiet and a little pale. She recovered somewhat when we hit the open road.

'They will be better off at the farm. They can get their families out when they are settled.'

'Anywhere is better than that shanty town.' said Renee, 'It was worse than I had ever imagined.'

I left the new workers by the tractor shed and went to find Samuel.

'Give them a tractor and one of your men to get started on a Nyumba. Make sure they have some food until they get paid and find them a place to sleep. I will square it with you on pay day.'

Soon the new men were settled in and at work on the site.

16

Kidney Stones

Digging started on the storage pits. I took some men off the phase two foundations to give the new men some impetus. I had planned to go down twelve feet which would require heaving the soil on to some staging with another team shovelling it the rest of the way, hard pick and shovel work. With enough people involved the first pit gradually took shape and one day it was finished. A peg and a piece of string with some trimming of the sides gave us a perfect circular hole.

Next a concrete floor was laid and a lining of four inch blocks was started; high tensile steel wire was laid every four courses and when the walling was finished it was cement rendered. To make sure of the strength, concrete was poured into the gap between the outer side of the blocks and the raw edge of the hole.

With all the work done the diggers came over to see the finished article. It had been a mammoth task, they were all proud to have been a part of it. I was very pleased with it also. A pipe was let into the walling on the lower side about a foot below the rim. This was the start of an overflow pipe which would lead to a similar holding pit on the perimeter of the unit. The bad news which I kept to myself was that our splendid work was to be repeated on the other side of phase two but this was for another day.

I had been watching progress on a large pig unit on the other side of Lusaka. Two farmers had taken over the pig business as a going concern to supplement their established farm. They were not really pig people and it seemed to me that they had served too many gilts for the available farrowing spaces and so it proved. They were anxious to sell off the surplus. It had always been my plan to import a nucleus of breeding stock but there was a need for some production to be generated meantime. I purchased enough pigs with suitable farrowing dates to fill our two farrowing houses.

Skottke had suggested that I go to South Africa at some stage for breeding stock. He put me in touch with a company in Pretoria called Fleiscentraal and we managed a telephone conversation. They sent a representative up to see me to discuss our possible future needs.

I planned to make the trip early in my third

year. Meantime I had to have a pigman in mind to look after the pigs when they arrived. Pondani expressed an interest. Perhaps he could see more permanence in the pig job or perhaps it was the wellie boots I had promised would go with the job. He had a brother who would work with him. My main concern at this point was that they should gradually gain experience in handling live-stock.

The gilts duly arrived. They were Large White/Landrace crosses, reared outside, covered in red soil and in good condition. Nkumba was now a pig farm.

Soon after this Skottke organised a group of farmers, representatives of machinery sellers and others with an interest in selling us medicines, insecticides and so on, to visit and view Nkumba now in the business of pig production. A large group assembled at the mill building where Skottke again explained our aims and, setting off in two parties we made an inspection. This was the start of Nkumba as a tourist attraction. We were obviously on the list of Zambian places to visit. We hosted several visits of parties and individuals from other African countries as well as the occasional minor Minister from European countries.

Meantime harvest was well under way, a

little late because we were awaiting our turn with the combine. We had started harvesting by hand mainly to get some maize in the store for the important visit. Eventually the combine was delivered from another of our farms and this caused some excitement and the harvest went on apace. The bulk storage was filling up; when this was full we would have grain to sell. The rains had tailed off a bit early and the yield was not as good as the first year but this was how it was, the crop yield depended largely on good rains.

The sunflower crop looked good with some heads nearly as big as dinner plates. I had been told that bees would arrive in numbers to work on the crop. To encourage this influx it seemed that empty oil drums or containers of any sort with an access slit cut in them would attract the bees. This seemed to work, indeed any hollow item with an access point would soon be busy with bees. It never occurred to me to wonder what function these makeshift hives performed; was it just overnight lodgings, and what happened to the pollen they collected? There was nothing left in the drums when, job done, they left.

The work of the bees could be clearly seen. Always working from the outside the outer edges were pollinated and started forming seeds. Ring by ring the heads would start making seeds, and then one day, work complete the bees left. The trick now was to harvest the crop when the seeds were ripe but before the heads drooped over and the seeds were shaken on to the ground. The combine was a great help in this respect gobbling up the crop in short order and straight to the bag. Hand harvesting would have shaken many seeds loose to fall on the ground.

It was a fine crop and I had learned that the stover was nutritious food for cattle. I had been toying with the idea of buying in a few head of cattle. They could graze for little or no cost in the bush. The only cost being for a couple of youngsters who would be engaged to herd them. At night they would come into a stockade to stop them wandering. They would be fed some sunflower stover and have available ad lib a molasses lick. Molasses was readily available from the Tate and Lyle sugar cane farms some miles to the south of us. I had seen how this was supplied to cattle. A trough was filled with molasses, the surface of the molasses was covered by a piece of plywood with one inch holes drilled at intervals. The plywood floated on the surface of the molasses until pushed down by the noses of the cattle when the molasses would come through the holes to be licked off by the cattle. This simple device prevented gorging but allowed a lick. Coupled with stover and bush grazing it seemed to be a tried and tested system. I was interested, especially as we had a long drinking trough and I had discovered a cattle dip grown over in the bush. Fly-born diseases were a hazard. It was one for the future.

★   ★   ★

It was towards the end of my second year that I became aware of paramilitary types driving around in lorries with no number plates. These became known as 'freedom fighters' and were training and were encamped in the bush near the Rhodesian border. Their purpose, to assist Rhodesia if independence was to be achieved by military means.

They were largely undisciplined and not above shooting the odd cow or other livestock for the cook pot. For the most part law abiding citizens avoided the border area. Nkumba, luckily, was far enough away from the border to be free from trouble from this source. Only the imprudent would chance their luck.

Renee was to be involved in two medical emergencies. One, the not infrequent rush to hospital with a too young girl in labour. It always seemed to happen late at night, I had the mattress ready at all times. This time Renee was with me as we rushed through a moonlit night with little time to spare. It was close to midnight when we handed over responsibility to the nursing staff. All was well, a baby was, we were informed later, born within forty minutes of our arrival at the hospital. What amazed Renee was the tableau we witnessed on the road the next afternoon; the husband was for once carrying the recently delivered baby with the wife padding along behind. They had walked twenty miles, it was about four in the afternoon when we saw them on the last leg of their journey. They had been walking for perhaps six hours which meant they would have set out around ten in the morning, so soon after the birth. This though was the norm; the hospital was under pressure for maternity beds; I was never asked to do the return journey for these young mothers which I would have been pleased to do. It was the way of life, what custom decreed, they never troubled me except in emergencies, and thank goodness they felt they could always call on me when their troubles were serious.

The next medical emergency was a rather sad affair involving a child. It appeared that Mahdi's house boy and wife had gone off on a drinking spree and had not returned the next day. They had left two children unattended, one girl about six years old and a boy somewhat younger. Renee was called by one of the women; the older girl had fallen in the cook fire which she had lit and was severely burned. She needed hospital treatment as soon as possible.

Lamek was despatched to find me and was unsuccessful but he did find Peter by the tractor shed. Renee asked Peter to take my pick-up which was in the yard and get the child to hospital. An hour later I returned from the fields with Samuel and Renee explained that she had despatched Peter in the pick-up to take a little girl to hospital. Well, I was able to report that the pick-up was still in the yard, Peter was nowhere to be seen. The child was in the tractor shed.

There seemed to be nothing for it but that we should get off to the hospital. We were a little apprehensive about this. We would much rather find a family member to go with us. In a situation like this we could easily be accused of not providing adequate care for the child or being responsible for the child's condition. I had in mind what the local police had told me about road accidents. They explained; if you have a road accident and someone is hurt, it does not matter who is to blame, if you stop to help, a crowd will gather and they could stone you. If you have an accident drive straight to the nearest police station. I had also seen one example of 'instant justice'. A policeman was leading a handcuffed man along a street in Lusaka; I was amazed to see passers by go up to the handcuffed man and punch him. This was Africa not UK we were just a little apprehensive; we would like to find a relative.

Lamek as usual was able to help. He knew of an uncle and was able to supply a name but no address. However, resourceful as ever he knew of this man's habits.

'He will be in a beer hall. He drinks a lot.'

'But which beer hall?'

Lamek gave us a choice of three. We set off and looked in on the drinking place we passed on trips to Chelston or Lusaka. It was a first visit to a beer hall for me, not an appetising experience but just about what I expected, dingy, gloomy and none too clean. Men stood about drinking, talking or arguing. They all stopped to stare when I walked in. I explained my mission to the man behind the bar. He called out and explained to all and sundry in voluble Chinyanja what my problem was. They gathered round, most seemed to know the man. Two of the beer halls on my list were mentioned. There seemed to be real concern for the little girl. I left, they returned to their drinking.

At the next beer hall we drew a blank but had better luck with our next port of call. A man came forward and introduced himself. 'I am the uncle. I come with you to the hospital. I will look after her.'

We left uncle and child at the hospital. A doctor told us that the child had extensive burns but was healthy. She would be alright but might need a lengthy stay in hospital. The uncle shook hands with us and thanked us for our help. We left it at that and headed back to the farm. Lamek said he had found someone in the compound who would look after the other child in the meantime. I had things to say to Peter.

Mahdi was angry with the houseboy and was all for sacking him but I pointed out that it would be the children who would suffer and there was the little one in hospital to think about. Mahdi came round to this way of thinking and agreed to give him a severe warning and a second chance. Renee and I had a look inside the Nyumba. There was no food, a few pieces of dried up tomato lay about the floor. This was the only case of neglect I came across; I hoped it would be the last.

I awoke one night with crippling pain in the area where the kidneys are located. Having had little reason to be aware of illness I was as ignorant of the cause as I had been about my earlier thrombosis. I had never experienced pain like it. I managed to get out of bed and on hands and knees crawled round to Renee's side of the bed. She was sleeping blissfully. I prodded her into wakefulness.

'I have this awful pain. I can hardly bear it.'

Renee was surfacing. 'Where is the pain?'

I indicated my lower back. Renee had never encountered kidney stones either so a diagnosis was not forthcoming. Between groans I asked for water. I seemed to have a great need to swallow quantities of water.

Renee was up and throwing on some clothes. 'You are going to hospital,' she said decisively. 'I shall go and get Mahdi.'

'Don't be too long. The pain is killing me.'

Renee rushed out to the pick-up. She tried to engage reverse gear, but unfamiliar with the steering column mounted gear lever, she was not having much luck. Agitation of mind and body was not helping. She appeared back in the bedroom. 'Where do I find reverse gear? I can't get the car out of the garage.'

Crouched on the floor, drinking water by the pint, pain had scattered my senses.

'I don't know,' I croaked. 'You'll just have to find it.'

Eventually she did get the car out of the garage and managed to find first gear. Happy that the car would now go forward she drove in first gear to Mahdi's house. Mahdi was quickly dressed and behind the wheel. I was loaded and sat hunched between them on the bench seat, a groaning, miserable wreck, consumed by this indescribable pain.

We tore along the dirt road and went even faster on the tarmac Great East Road. We had passed Chelston and were nearing our destination when we came upon a scene of utter carnage. Wrecked cars at crazy angles, bodies being laid out by the roadside, gesticulating policemen everywhere. A multiple pileup; dead bodies, no doubt many injured; the hospital would have its hands full. In any case the road would not be cleared for many hours. Mahdi was explaining our situation to a policeman and showing signs of frustration. Renee was sitting quiet and withdrawn. Suddenly I realised the pain had gone. 'The pain has gone,' I announced.

Mahdi broke off his dialogue with the policeman and glared. 'What do you mean, the pain has gone. You give us all this trouble and now you say the pain has gone.'

'Well it has.' I said. 'Completely. I feel fine.'

I sensed Renee's relief when she clasped my hand and said quietly, 'We can go home now.'

It seemed that the kidney stone which had given me so much agony had passed into my bladder. This was dealt with by a one-day stay in hospital.

Mr Bird the surgeon said they had been busy treating kidney stones lately. 'Must be something in the water,' he said grinning. 'We'll fix you up.'

Of course they did. I was sick in Independence Avenue on the way home and that was that.

17

Kafue Game Park

On October 24th 1965 Kenneth Kaunda was appointed President of independent Zambia. Simon Kapwepwe was appointed Vice President. The University of Zambia was opened in Lusaka in 1966. Among other institutions established was the Evelyn Hone College of applied Arts and Commerce. This fine college was the home of the Lusaka Chess Club.

Another feature of the Kaunda reign was to take a 51%, sometimes more, share in foreign owned businesses including the mining companies. Secure in his Presidency since 1965, by the 1970's he was beginning to worry about competition. In 1972 he somehow persuaded Tom Nkumbula to wind up his A.N.C. party and join up with his own U.N.I.P. party. This left Simon Kapwepwe who had decided to leave U.N.I.P. and had founded a rival party, The United Progressive Party. Kapwepwe had to be removed.

How this was achieved is not quite clear. The story that filtered through to my rural situation was that a 6am raid picked up all

The United Progressive Party members. Their fate was not reported. We could only guess at a period of confinement. Whatever the real facts of the matter, there was one item closer to home I knew to be correct; a young man working in our headquarters in Lusaka was approached by two policemen, lifted bodily from his chair and dragged away. No information as to his subsequent treatment was available. He never in my time returned to work. The word in the office was that his only misdemeanour was to attend Simon Kapwepwe's rallies.

There was now a One Party Participatory Democracy. The Kaunda Philosophy was 'humanism'; One Party, One State was a slogan often quoted but in October 1991 a stunning defeat left Kaunda out in the cold to be replaced by Frederick Chiluba. Multi party politics returned and I think I saw somewhere that Simon Kapwepwe was again involved. This was long after I had left the country.

Some time after Zambia became a one party state I met Tom Nkumbula at a farmhouse Sunday lunch party, a pleasant, elderly man. We did not talk politics, we exchanged pleasantries, shook hands and that was all. It occurred to me to wonder, not for the first time why anyone ever went into politics.

We had indulged ourselves down on the site by making steel roof trusses for the service house. While this was now well within the expertise of our workshop lads and looked very smart, painted with a yellow rust inhibitor, I decided not to repeat the experiment as it was rather costly. Indeed when we repeated the building on phase two I used gum poles to make the roof trusses.

The first service area was finished and awaiting its first customers and the dry sow accommodation was practically ready. I still had in mind to go south early in my third year to buy breeding stock. There would be a large number of maiden gilts. I would have to plan for their housing. I went for simplicity. A long building divided into two parts. A water trough all the way along one wall, a brick cemented in at one end to ensure a four and a half inch depth of water. The trough would be dead level end to end; a tap would drip water continually, this to be adjusted to ensure a constant supply of water but without undue overflow. Two large outdoor paddocks would be part walled, part fenced. Gilts would have free access to the paddocks. This gilt section would supply both sections of the unit. It was my intention to operate phase one and phase two as separate units each with its own staff. There would of course be sensible co-operation between the two units and gilts would be drawn from a common pool as required.

The bigger gilts would be selected and occupy one house; a boar would be introduced. The second part of the housing would have smaller gilts but when appropriate a boar would be introduced here. There would be no recording of service dates; very simply, as gilts began to show udder development they would be removed to a farrowing house. I had no plans for sophisticated management as used in U.K.; induced farrowing of batches to ensure maximum use of expensive buildings or early weaning to get more litters per year. This was a different ball game. Housing was not expensive, water was free, labour ridiculously cheap; there was no pressure on land or space and of course the system had to suit the inexperienced workers and the variable nature of the ingredients available to make pig feed. Housing therefore had to be sufficient to cope with slower growth rate but with such a benign climate there was no need for controlled environment houses with complicated heating and ventilation, heat exchange units and the likes. So a simple, somewhat old fashioned system which was manageable by my trainee staff was the aim. Water bills on an intensive U.K. unit with the dependence on frequent pressure washing, could be enormous. Our borehole never let us down.

With pigs in some of the buildings and slurry channels working I began to think of slurry disposal. I had in mind a slurry pump with pipes taking slurry out to the land where a 'rain gun' would spray the stuff around. This plan didn't get off the ground initially as there were no slurry pumps to be bought. It would mean importing, a lengthy wait and expensive to boot. I then had another idea. We could make a slurry spreader.

I got quite excited about this and asking around I was able to buy a lorry chassis on quite good tyres. Next I had a tank rolled at Chilanga Cement. This we mounted on the chassis. Next a pipe out the back leading to a boom with holes drilled at intervals. An impeller pump was located in the pipe from the tank with a Briggs and Stratton engine to drive it. The slurry would be pumped into the boom at pressure, and would be forced through the holes. It didn't work. Despite increasing the hole sizes, the slurry refused to co-operate and blocked up the holes very effectively. After further experimentation I had to admit defeat. However defeat was not total. By removing the boom and fitting an upright pipe with a curved piece at the top we had a very efficient water bowser.

I had always been aware that a failure of our borehole or repairs to the pump might result in a crisis. Now with a large tank of water at the ready and header tanks on each building, I had, however inadvertently, secured the unit against water shortages. However a water bowser did nothing to resolve the problem of slurry disposal. I went back to A.F.E. where my original approaches had been made and asked if they could make up a tractor mounted, power take off driven pump. I suggested a 'Mono Pump' which consisted of a rubber housing shaped to take a rotating metal screw. Yes of course they could do this, why had we not come up with this idea before? Why indeed?

★　★　★

The harvest was over; the barn storage was full, and John and Trish had arrived for their holidays. It was great to be all together again. The highlight was to be a visit to the Kafue Game Park. Ben Van Kuringen had offered to take us in his Combi. Meantime the family played table tennis, spent some time helping on the site as before and once in a while we would take an afternoon family walk in the bush.

It was on one of these occasions that I spotted a snake resting on a tree. It was the type of snake that was hard to distinguish from a thin branch or a twig. Whether it was venomous or not I had no idea. Trish was up ahead, I could see she would pass quite close to the snake, I called out, 'keep walking Trish.' She cleared the snake by about a yard. When I pointed it out she was a bit shocked. For the rest of the holiday I only had to call, 'keep walking Trish,' for her to stiffen with fright. She was also not too keen on the crickets which chirped in the roof space.

I had been a bit wary of walking in the bush in my early days, but soon realised that snakes were equipped to hear you coming and got out of the way. The greatest risk would be in the early morning when snakes were sluggish after a cool night. If you had the bad luck to step on, say, a puff adder warming up in the sun it would most likely result in a bite. These cold blooded reptiles needed to warm up to become fully operational. Once their mobility was restored they would keep out of the way.

I surprised a green mamba one day lurking in my geraniums. It must have been six feet long; it took off at speed round the corner of the house. I saw a black mamba one day. It crossed the farm road in front of me; I stopped to let it pass. The only death from snake bite I heard of was the sad case of a young student who was riding his scooter along a wet main road. He spotted a black mamba crossing and swerved to avoid it. Unfortunately in doing so his bike skidded; he landed by the snake and was bitten on the head. He died before any help could get to him.

One day driving along the farm road a cobra reared up on the verge. The farm road was narrow and I had to pass quite close to it. I quickly wound up my window and had a fine view of this very fine snake. Its face was on a level with the bottom of my window, I don't know how much was coiled down below. There was another variety of the cobra, the spitting cobra. This one would spit venom at the eyes of the victim and was reported to be accurate at a range of fifteen feet. I did hear of one instance where someone fell foul of one of the spitters. I knew her; she ran some pigs at their home, her husband managed one of big stores in Lusaka.

The lady saw a snake enter her house. She searched everywhere but could not find it. In the bathroom she was aware that part of the bath panel had been missing for some time. Perhaps it was in there? Rather unwisely she looked in. The cobra spat its venom. She spent the night in hospital having her eyes bathed at intervals. She made a full recovery. I never heard what happened to the snake. Perhaps it made good its escape but it is more likely that someone despatched it.

I never encountered a Boomslang or a Python. Boomslangs could be found usually above your head, coiled round a tree branch. I did hear of a python which had invaded someone's hen run. Having taken on board perhaps more than one hen, the bulge prevented it escaping through the hole through which it had entered. It was still there in the morning and apparently paid the penalty for its lack of foresight. It was reported to be nine feet long.

★ ★ ★

We all piled into Ben's Combi. We were off to the game park, all set to do some game spotting. The journey was uneventful, we passed small settlements, some just a collection of Nyumbas. There was the odd roadside Coca Cola stall or a barber cutting hair by the roadside but for the most part it was scrub bush and dirt roads with brown the predominant colour. It was the dry season; we had the usual dusty ride. I had noticed that the trees started to green up some weeks before the rains were due. Did they respond to a rise in temperature which, with much increased humidity happened in October. I never did resolve this one.

We passed through one little town or perhaps it was just a big village with shops. We drove along the main street. 'Just like a wild west town in the old films,' was John's verdict and indeed it was. The town was called Mumbwa; the main street was wide and dusty, either side lined with wooden houses and shops in varying states of dilapidation. A wild west style covered board walk on either side of the street sheltered pedestrians from the sun. All it needed was some tumbleweed blowing in the wind, some lounging cowboys and a few tethered horses. In fact there were few people about; those who were stood and stared.

We arrived at the game park. An elderly official checked our credentials, sprayed around our vehicle with a flit spray and waved us through. We followed the road to the camp where we had booked our accommodation. We arrived and took stock. Our sleeping huts were oblong in shape, solidly built with thatched roofs. There was a central area with the remnants of a wood fire in the middle and seats clustered round and what looked like a cookhouse a little way off. We saw a bit more when the man in charge showed us round.

The huts were simply but adequately furnished and there were mosquito nets over the beds. John was not over happy about this indicator of a biting fly nuisance. I explained that we were in mosquito territory and also in the province of the one which caused sleeping sickness. John was not impressed when I explained the symptoms, probably without real medical knowledge, not very accurately. I suggested that if he were to be infected he might feel sleepy, listless, lethargic. John, not very keen on flies and their effects, responded. 'I wouldn't know whether I had it or not. I feel like that a lot of the time anyway.'

We had brought our own meat in a cool box. It was now in one of a row of fridges and would be prepared for us on request, by the camp cook when we returned from our game spotting. Other food was supplied by the cookhouse as required. We were too late in the day to go game spotting so we rested up. A large campfire was being prepared in the central area and as darkness approached a generator kicked into life and our lights came on. After our meal we joined others round the campfire for conversation and a comparing of notes, where they saw lions, zebra, giraffe and so on. There is always a life and soul of the party type in any gathering and someone tried to jolly things up with a sing song. A few joined in but it soon fizzled out and people were back to comparing notes.

We were obviously near the Kafue river because I heard the unmistakable grunting and splashing of hippos. They would no doubt have been grazing somewhere on dry land. I had been told never to get between grazing hippos and the river because if they were startled there would be a cavalry charge for the security of the water. They would take a direct line and would not be inclined to sidestep any unwary human who had strayed into their path. Having said that, I never saw hippos anywhere but immersed in the river. John had obviously heard the animal noises and was looking nervously over his shoulder. I reassured him that they would be at least a mile away then spoiled it by relaying the information about not getting in their way. It was John who suggested we might have an early night.

We were up with the lark the next morning and having breakfasted were soon on our way. The game seemed thin on the ground; in the first four hours we had spotted some waterbuck, a few wildebeest, quite a lot of impala but none of the big boys. The afternoon drive did produce a pair of lions and some kudu but no elephants. In fact the week passed and we never did see an elephant. We did manage a sighting of giraffe, a small herd of buffalo and a few zebra. It was all a bit disappointing; game seemed to be in short supply. We had driven miles each day often for hours without seeing anything. What we did see were in small numbers. On the other hand the accommodation was good, we kept the Combi free of flies by liberal use of fly spray and Ben, bless him, did all the driving.

★　★　★

Having been concerned with avoiding fly contact for a week I was aware that flies were becoming troublesome on the unit. We had the usual trays of fly bait suspended from the ceiling but they were only partially successful. But help was at hand. A salesman of my acquaintance came up with an offer. His company had a quantity of insecticide which had been partially damaged by seawater, enough for it to be not saleable in the normal way. He quoted a giveaway price for what he estimated to be about half a tonne. I wanted to be sure it would kill flies and was soluble. He reassured me on those points and we had a deal.

This was the start of a virtually fly free unit, a rare thing in Zambia. I purchased two knapsack sprayers and had two men spray the insides of the roofs throughout the unit as a first job each morning. At this early hour the flies were clustered on the inside of the roofs and a maximum kill was achieved. As time went on the fly population decreased and we reached a stage where we were hardly aware of flies. I am sure the pigs appreciated their disappearance.

★ ★ ★

The family experienced several facets of Zambian weather. They also missed some, like a typical African thunderstorm. These firework displays had to be seen to be believed. Crashing thunder and lightning, almost continuous, the noise indescribable. Then rain on the corrugated iron roof adding to the tumult. I do not remember a storm during the daylight hours. I was glad to be sheltered by a fairly substantial house; what it was like in the grass thatched Nyumbas in the compound I could only guess at. However the family were intrigued to see tumbleweed blowing across the ploughed land and the mini whirlwinds scurrying across the fields lifting columns of dry soil. Come to think of it they missed the big one which tore through the piggery one night. We arrived at work in the morning to find that a path some fifteen feet wide had been very efficiently cleaved through part of the piggery. The whirlwind had hit the first fattening house, taking with it walls and roof of a section as neatly as if a J.C.B. had been hired to do the job. It repeated the performance on the second fattening house then veered off to leave its mark on the dry sow house. Debris was scattered over a wide area. Roofing sheets especially had been carried perhaps half a mile. This was the only big one I experienced or even heard of. Once again I wondered at the consequences of such a freakish wind tearing through the compound. It was a blessing also that that there were no pigs in the houses at the time. If the wind was strong enough to tear down concrete block walls it would surely have taken the pigs for a ride had they been housed. Flying pigs — the mind boggles.

The family did witness a bush fire, not an infrequent occurrence. This one was not threatening any of our crops. We had a good view from our bungalow as it raced past some hundred yards away. A sufficient cleared area around the house and also round the compound, maintained at all times, kept us safe. We were not surrounded by the fire; the bush was all to one side of us but the compound would have been surrounded at some point.

With the wind behind them the fires would travel at considerable speed, the flames devouring undergrowth and shooting up trees to strip them of leaves and smaller branches, leaving behind blackened trunks. It was remarkable how quickly the trees recovered.

Only once was I faced with a fire which threatened a crop. The alarm was raised and everyone seemed to know what was required. Samuel had a man on a tractor with a mounted plough on its way to the danger in next to no time.

'We know what to do,' he said.

'Good,' I said, 'you are in charge.'

Men piled into my pick-up armed with sacks, shovels, tree branches, anything that could be used to beat out any threat to the crop. We lined up along the headland, which was wide and intended as a fire break. The fire would not cross but embers or flaming twigs blowing in the wind could start a fire in the maize which would race through like wildfire. If anything did drop in the crop the beaters would be on to it. If a fire broke out the man on the tractor would plough round it at high speed to encircle it and stop it spreading.

I was quite apprehensive as a great wall of fire roared towards us. The trees were quite tall and the fire seemed to loom over us as the action started. The heat was terrific and there was an angry roar from the fire as battle was engaged. Twice, fires broke out in the maize but our tractor man was round them in a trice. Beaters, including myself, rather sweaty by now, kept flying embers under control. The wide fire break did the rest and quite suddenly the fire gave up. All fell silent except for the chatter of the beaters. The maize was saved.

The first rains always came as a cause for celebration; not only because the land was being watered but, after such a long dry spell, with each day exactly like the next except for a rise in temperature and humidity in October, we had had enough of wall to wall sunshine. So that thunderous hammering on the roof was a welcome sound. Of course the rains could bring with it problems but the deep ploughed land could soak up the rain like a sponge, and there was still hot sunshine to dry up the surface. Work on the site was not much affected. There was one occasion

169

when I was caught out after an hour of torrential rain. I set off in my pick-up down the farm road. I saw water lying further down the road. I had no reason to think it was anything more than surface water. I drove into it and suddenly the nose of the car dropped into a deep hole. Water flowed past on either side. There was nothing for it but to escape through a window, take a photograph and walk back to the farm for help. The cause of the trouble was a small stream which was piped under the road, but when the stream became a torrent the whole lot was washed away. When the water subsided there was a great hole in the road. Pulled out by a tractor, the pickup, dried out by a spell in the sun, started up and appeared to have escaped any damage.

I was always a bit careful thereafter about water collected on a road. My caution paid dividends when after a similar heavy downpour I was leaving the Nel's farm. There were three roads leading out of the farm. I chose one and came across a dip which was holding water. I edged in carefully to test the depth. I soon realised that there probably was enough water to completely submerge my pick-up. I hastily reversed and chose one of the other roads.

I heard a story which brought home to me

the vital function of the rainy season. A man appeared on the site one day when we had moved on and had store pigs which we were growing on to bacon weight. The man introduced himself as a dairy farmer and he wanted to buy a pig to feed on for domestic consumption. I had heard of this man and his fine herd of Friesian cows. 'How did you get into cows?' I asked.

'Well, it's a long story,' he replied.

'Go on, I'd like to hear it?'

'I was an accountant in South Africa. A good job, well paid, I had accumulated some capital.'

'So you bought your first cow,' I suggested.

'It was some time before I bought my first cow,' he smiled, 'but the time did come. First though I came up here and bought a farm. Land was cheap, I planted a crop of maize, and guess what?'

'You became rich overnight,' I guessed.

'Rather the opposite. The rains started then failed completely. Just enough rain to get the maize started, then no more, the sprouting maize just withered and died.'

'So you went back down south to recoup?' I offered.

'No, but that was one option. The other was to plant another crop. I had just enough money left to do this. I planted another crop the following November, the rains this time were good. I had a bumper harvest. Later I thought that milk production suited me better but it all started with one good rainy season.'

He went off with a pig in the boot of his car. I was left to ponder the fickle nature of the rains.

★   ★   ★

A column of marching ants is a sight to behold. Six to eight inches wide, very orderly with big headed soldier ants in the van. Where have they come from? Where are they going? Only they know. Perhaps they are looking for new feeding grounds or are off to establish new territory. No doubt with as much purpose as armies in our past history with columns of soldiers setting off to conquer foreign lands.

All very well in a bush situation but when I saw that my kitchen was a target of one such column I was horrified. Obviously the ant course round the house was a deterrent but there was always the open door. As they advanced at a steady pace, Lamek, ever resourceful, arrived with a broom. Vigorous sweeping and floor washing did the trick on this occasion and it was after this encounter that I realised that petrol could divert the course of a march.

I had to use it in earnest one night as we prepared for bed. Renee spotted a trickle of ants coming in through the bedroom window. Somehow they had evaded the mesh screen coming either through or under it. I had a knapsack sprayer and some petrol on hand and rushed outside to deal with the incoming marchers. Inside, some vigorous dustpan and brush work completed the victory. For some time Renee went to sleep sitting up with the light on and the window under observation. I was a little disappointed that the ant course did not deter the invasion and wondered if it was more ornamental than effective.

The third invasion happened one evening in the piggery. The night watchman raised the alarm. Ants had entered one building. I recruited our son and each with a knapsack filled with petrol we set off to clear the decks and repel further boarders. I had heard horror stories of ants getting up the noses of pigs and driving them mad. Luckily the ants had not advanced beyond the dunging passage. We set to work and soon had the house cleared and the column diverted away from our livestock.

Termites, often referred to as white ants could be equally damaging. If they entered a house, say, when the occupants were away, they would eat everything from account books to the contents of the wardrobes. A jacket or shirt left inadvertently in a field would be tidied up by morning. I discovered that the fence posts round my garden were hollowed out leaving only the bark. However termites' progress could be seen, since being unable to survive in the light, they build little tunnels to get to their food supply. Despite this restriction they are everywhere. A dead animal dragged into the bush would be reduced to bones by the next morning. Luckily there were efficient dusting powders to protect stored grain and the like. Perhaps the most impressive thing about termites is the sometimes towering rock-like structure that is their home. Sometimes a group of such can be found, sometimes a single one only. It is quite remarkable that such tiny creatures, unable to function in sunlight can fashion such a solid fortress home. However, they flourish and do a good job keeping the bush litter free.

★　★　★

Holidays don't go on for ever. The family would soon be gone but I would rather have foregone the events that preceded their departure. Renee was out walking with Meg. She followed a familiar route, across a field then along a path through a narrow strip of bush which offered some shade. She was well used to this route which passed close to the building site and led on to the farm road. On this occasion she was accosted by a youth who wrestled her to the ground. Poor old Meg, once so brave, stood by bewildered by this turn of events. Renee fought her assailant and bit his hand. Things, no doubt would have turned out badly had a group of people not arrived on the scene. The youth ran off and Renee arrived at the bungalow in a state of shock. I had been away that day and arrived back as darkness was falling. I came back to a family in distress. I was furious. It was surely not one of my lads. A stranger; but who? Renee described the youth. He would be about eighteen, tall, wearing khaki shirt and shorts. 'He will have teeth marks on his hand. I gave him a good hard bite.'

This was a clue. I grabbed my shotgun and headed for the compound. I called at each Nyumba, frightening the life out of some as I suddenly appeared in the firelight. At each Nyumba I demanded to see the whole family and explained who I was looking for and why. I wanted to spread the word far and wide. I sought out John Tembo. He had recently been training, in his own time, to be an auxiliary policeman.

'We start early tomorrow John. We will visit every village and compound for miles. We will find this youth.'

'Yes Bwana,' John was ready for some police work. 'I take you to all the Nyumbas I know.'

Our hunt started at first light. One of my employees was squatting on some land just outside our boundary. He had some extended family and they had four Nyumbas. He also had a cow and some cultivated land. I demanded that they all assemble for inspection. The gun I carried — unloaded in case of accidents — and my angry voice, plus an auxiliary policeman by my side brooked no resistance. We drew a blank. We moved on and entered another cluster of huts. A small boy was seated by a fire, a pile of dead rats by his side. He was singeing the hair off them and scraping them with a knife. We had no luck here and so the hunt went on for two days, and then there was a development. Renee had a phone call from the local police. 'We need you to come to the police station. A boy has come here and says you beat him. You must come right away.'

To say that Renee was upset would be an understatement but by the time she had despatched Lamek to find me and I had arrived post haste, she had been in touch with the British High Commission. She had been promised a call back and this came as I arrived. It was the High Commissioner on the phone. Renee explained in detail her problem and her fears.

The High Commissioner listened carefully, then suggested a meeting on the Great East Road. We would go together to the police station. He was waiting as promised.

'Give me your passport,' he said to Renee. 'I won't let them have that.'

At the police station the interrogation started. This was taking place in a corridor; people were passing to and fro. Renee was distraught, the High Commissioner was getting angry.

'I demand we have a proper interview in a private room,' he said. We went into an office. 'Now, your story.'

The police were somewhat disconcerted by this high up authority figure. 'This boy says Madam beat him but we can find no marks on him.'

'Does he have a bite mark on his hand?'

'Yes he does.'

'Then I will give you the facts. This boy must be punished.' Our protector was not prepared to mess about.

'Then Madam must make charges; take the boy to court.'

Renee said. 'I am not staying. I will leave as soon as I can get a flight.'

'Then we will deal with him in our own way.' What that would be we could only guess.

Soon a night flight carried my family back to the U.K. A sad and unfortunate end to a holiday. The youth was not one of ours but he had been sheltering in the Nyumbas just off our land. We should have been more ruthless and searched the Nyumbas. As it was I sacked the man who had protected the miscreant. Everyone knew why he was going. Justice as I saw it was done.

Time passed. Renee reported she was back at work. Life moved on.

18

Elephants

One of my strict rules was that I did not want anybody knocking on my door before seven on a Sunday morning; except of course, in an emergency. I had for a few weeks been instructing a few interested building workers on the use of the Kern Kwickset level. This little group would assemble around seven and wait patiently until I appeared. It was then with some irritation that I woke one Sunday morning to a considerable amount of noise and insistent hammering on my door.

An excited group were assembled. 'Elephants Bwana', they all seemed to shout at once. I could well understand their excitement. They had almost certainly never seen a sight like this and these huge specimens could so easily walk through their relatively flimsy Nyumbas. By now I was quite excited. I dressed quickly. 'How many?'

'Eight Bwana, very big.'

'I shall follow them and see where they go. I need one man who knows the bush.'

A man stepped forward.

'Don't worry, we won't let them get to the compound,' I said to the assembled company. They smiled and clapped their hands.

We set off, my guide taking me to where the elephants had been sighted. A herd of eight leave an easy trail to follow. Trampled bushes, the odd tree pulled down to get at its fruits, broken branches, the elephant is not kind to its environment. The fairly regular occurrence of large heaps of dung, still steaming, with dung flies arriving, indicated that the herd was not far ahead. The hard outer casing of some kind of large fruit which I could not identify was present, undigested in the dung, indicating the feeding preference for the day.

We had been following the trail for two hours without a sighting. Making our way across a dried up wadi with elephant grass over head high was a disconcerting experience. I felt that we could be only yards away from an elephant and not be aware of it. But no, the trail went on, the morning passed, we had walked miles. I was counting on my guide to get us back to the farm. We had not talked much; his English was limited.

I asked, 'which way the farm?'

He looked around him, hesitated and pointed. I was not totally convinced. I started to worry.

'We may as well press on,' I said. I really did want to see the elephants.

It was two in the afternoon when I began to feel that the bush was somehow familiar. We were still following the elephants' trail. Then we were clear of the bush and in a field. I recognised one of our fields, I heaved a sigh of relief. The elephants had crossed the field. We followed their tracks. We came to a stream which cut through the field between two high banks. We looked down. Below us the elephants were drinking, waggling their ears and apparently content to stay in their valley enjoying the stream and the shade of surrounding trees.

I got my pick-up out and drove to Christie Nel's place. I asked if he would like to see some elephants.

'Leave the gun at home of course,' I said.

'They are safe enough. I don't have a licence for an elephant. I never break the rules or the ethics. Never shoot an in-calf female for instance.' He grinned. 'Let's go.'

Diane came as well. We sat on the bank watching the elephants disporting themselves below.

'They are young,' said Christie, 'not much tusk, male, a group of young bachelors. It sometimes happens. The dominant male won't let them near the females to mate. They may lurk around the periphery of the herd hoping to nab a female when the old chap's not looking. More often or not they club up like these fellows. Later they may challenge a dominant male, meantime they eat, drink and fart. A bit like a rugby club really.'

'Of course someone might shoot them first,' I suggested.

'The law of the jungle,' said Christie grinning. He took some biltong from his pocket, sharpened his knife on his boot and cut off a wad. 'Have some,' he offered.

I declined, having tried this sun cured meat on another occasion.

'Good job they found the water here. There's that big cattle trough in the compound. Lucky they found this first.'

The elephants stayed with us for a week, setting off on feeding forays in the early morning, returning to their stream in the afternoon. And then one day they moved on. In a way I was sorry to see them go. I think I was the only one.

★ ★ ★

John Tembo came back from Chilanga Cement. He looked upset. 'No cement Bwana.' I couldn't believe it, a cement works without cement. 'How long before they catch up?'

'Two weeks Bwana. But they have plenty of lime.'

Two weeks could mean three; I was worried. I had to keep the builders building. This was a crisis. I was in bed that night racking my brains when I had the glimmer of an idea. They had plenty of lime. Old buildings were held together with lime mortar. I would be wary of using it in the pig buildings but I could build some decent houses for the workers.

But how to knock up this lime mortar. The next day I was in the library in Lusaka. I found a very old book which had a recipe for lime mortar. I got back to the farm and sent John Tembo off for a load of lime.

We cleared an area near the piggery and before our cement ran out we prepared concrete slabs on which to build our houses. Next, following the instructions in the old book we knocked up some lime mortar. This required slaking and mixing and a period of maturing and more mixing but we finally had some building mortar. The plan was for two rooms, one on either side of a connecting, open fronted porch. I wanted to put a fireplace and chimney in this space but Sunday held up his hands in horror.

'No, No, Bwana they always cook outside.

This space is for maize, a bicycle, firewood, not for cooking.'

I could see Sunday's point of view. I had seen Peter's mother cooking outside the large old farmhouse which housed Peter's family members. I once had occasion to call at Lamek's house. There was a fireplace in his porch and it was occupied by a broody hen sitting on eggs.

So, thanks to a plentiful supply of lime and a very old building book I kept the site working. In the new building plan I had included a wash house. This was a long building with a concrete floor and drainage. A water supply was laid on consisting of a pipe running through the building above head height with taps at intervals to use for showering. I also provided a toilet which was the usual hole in the concrete floor with a tap and a piece of hose for washing down, but down below was a proper septic tank arrangement with a soak away pipe. It seemed to work alright; I was again working from the old book.

I was pleased with my efforts at rural housing development and a little peeved when there didn't seem to be any competition from potential occupants. I guessed they were settled in the compound and unwilling to move out to suburbia. I had plans to recruit some extra labour and put on an afternoon shift, they would be able to move right in.

Chilanga took nearly four weeks to catch up with demand. We had some catching up to do ourselves. A few more site workers were needed to compensate for workers being moved over to cope with the demands of the pigs. I could see a time at the end of the contract when the new housing would be occupied by piggery workers at which time the compound would revert to a few Nyumbas occupied by arable workers.

19

Bandits

I heard news of a farmer who was selling up after being attacked by bandits. The word was that he had some good quality sows to sell. I thought it was worth looking into, so I made arrangements to visit. The farm was twenty miles or so up the Great North Road. I was devastated by what I found there. The farmer still carried the bruises resulting from the severe beating he had sustained. He invited me in. The whitewashed walls were streaked with blood. Every room carried evidence of the brutality of the attack, bloodstains on floors and walls, broken furniture, smashed windows; I could see that the farmer and his wife were lucky to be alive.

The farmer told me how events had unfolded. 'My wife's in Lusaka, with friends, they damaged her back.' He paused for a moment then went on. 'I was selling vegetables in Lusaka, that's where it started. They followed me home, thought I had a lot of cash on me.'

'But you had banked it?' I knew Christie

Nel, who also sold vegetables off the back of his truck in Lusaka kept popping the money into the bank.

'Yes, it doesn't pay to keep money on you. I had only a small amount on me. Of course they didn't believe me. I gave them what I had but they were not satisfied; they were angry.'

'So then the beating started. You and your wife must have thought you were going to die.'

'One had a shotgun, the others had sticks. There were four of them. The beatings went on. We ran into other rooms, they followed; we cowered against the walls, trying to protect our heads with our arms; that's where most of the blood on the walls came from. We were close to passing out, then we managed to escape to the bathroom.

There was a lock on the door, we would be safe until they broke it down. At least we had a breather. There was a small window. I shouted through the window as if my workers were nearby. 'Help, bring machetes, sticks, spears.' I called names as if I could see my workers. 'We have bandits, come and drive them off.'

'Did it work?'

'Yes, they seemed to fall for it or maybe they realised there was no more money in the

187

house. They left. We patched up our wounds as best we could then I got my wife to the hospital. They dressed our sores properly, luckily nothing broken but my wife will need nursing care for a while. She will never live out here again. Nothing for it but to sell up.'

It was a sad story. We went to look at the pigs. He ran a small herd of sows. I purchased a few good quality sows one of which was to win the top awards at Lusaka Show the following year. I left saddened by what I had seen, reflecting on the poverty and lack of jobs; of the hunger and living conditions in the shanty towns which must be at the root of much of the banditry, thieving, pick pocketing, and crime in general which was rife in the towns and cities of Zambia at that time.

So much better, I felt, to live in bush situations. My crew for instance had clean water to drink, regular work, a housing situation they were used to and a community where people helped each other.

The sows were delivered early the next morning. Most livestock movement was done before the sun was up. In open lorries the hot sun soon caused distress to animals and pigs in particular suffer in high temperatures.

With a pig farm now in operation I thought a visit to the veterinary centre in Lusaka would not come amiss. The veterinary service was free and since I had been obliged to take pigs from different environments there might be veterinary problems of one sort and another. There would be another influx of pigs when I went on a buying spree to South Africa which I still hoped to do in the early part of my final year. There would be a settling down period after which I would hope to close the herd to outside influences.

At the veterinary centre I met Larvs Larsen, a Dane, who said he would like to come out and have a look round. 'Would you like to see some rabid dogs?' he asked.

'Yes as long as they can't get at me,' I said.

'Come.' We entered a row of pens with barred fronts. In each pen there was a dog.

'They will be put down and their brains will be examined for signs of rabies,' explained Larvs. With his foot he pushed a food dish under the bars of one pen. The dog snarled and pounced on the dish.

I had seen enough. 'Let's go,' I said. I was glad Meg had been injected against rabies. Larvs was to become a good friend and supplied any veterinary input we needed.

★ ★ ★

Planting time soon came round again. The rains had started well and growth was rapid.

So good in fact that it became obvious that Mahdi was not going to get all the fertiliser on in time, and so it proved. Tractor work had to be suspended. I consulted Skottke about some help from our aircraft. He said he would see what he could do but the plane was pretty busy. He must have gone to an outside contractor but a plane had been organised. When it arrived I thought it looked a bit like a World War I plane with cylinders surrounding the propeller. Out of it stepped a young Canadian.

'Was the landing strip OK.?' I asked.

'Just about. I'll manage,' he grinned. 'We get used to bumpy landings.'

Most farms maintained a landing strip. Ours was long, right across a field but it also doubled as a fire break. The criterion was; if you can drive your car along it at sixty miles an hour it will do.

Fertilising started. I went on leave. When I returned I discovered that the plane had crashed in the bush. I inspected the burnt out plane which stood on its nose. All the fabric was gone but the blackened metal framework remained intact. The pilot apparently had stepped out unharmed but for a few bruises. So what went wrong?

It was reported that the fully loaded plane had set off flying over ground that had a steady upward slope. The plane seemed to be unable to gain height to compensate for the rising ground and so flew into the bush at the end of the field at tree top level, fouled a tall tree and crashed. Why had it not been able to gain height? Perhaps because it was over-loaded. But why should it be overloaded? He put the same amount in each time. What could have happened was that he had not fully emptied his tank on several forays and these accumulated until unfortunately, when he did an uphill run he was overloaded. The company plane had to come in to finish the job.

This was only the second time our landing strip had been used. The other time was when a young Englishman landed his light plane to ask directions to the Chalambana Dairy Project. I drove him up to the house for a cup of tea before setting him off in the right direction.

★   ★   ★

Larvs Larsen and I were soon firm friends. He had been out to look round the pig unit and on another occasion needed a subject on which to try out a drug which was new to him. The drug was immobolin which when injected rendered the subject unconscious until an antidote was administered. I had a pig with a large umbilical rupture which would benefit from a repair.

Larvs came out. We improvised an operating table with empty oil drums and a sheet of chipboard. The drug was very efficient but at the same time quite dangerous. I made sure I knew that the antidote was on hand and that I knew how to use it in the event of Larvs having an accident. We held the pig firmly as he made his injection. The pig was asleep immediately and Larvs set about repairing the hernia. There was no danger that the pig would wake up. The job done and the antidote injected, the pig was soon back with us, repaired and ready to be placed in an isolation pen well bedded with maize stover where it would quite quickly be fully recovered.

And so Larvs became part of our pig set up. I was also indebted to him for attendance on our elderly dog when she became poorly. One evening Meg was showing symptoms of abdominal pain. I set off with her to find Larvs in Lusaka. At the time he lived in a block of flats. I knew where to find this building, I went inside, there was not a soul about, it was dimly lit and a bit creepy. Luckily a young couple appeared returning home from an outing. Yes they knew where the Vet lived; they were able to give me the floor and his number. I knocked on the door. There was no response; either Larvs was out or he did not for security reasons answer his door after dark. I waited but eventually had to leave.

Meg was in pain, whimpering and obviously distressed. I had to do something. Back at the farm I took stock of available medicines. I thought engemycin might do the trick. I decided to try the intravenous route using a vein in the foreleg but without assistance this defeated me. An injection under the skin was the only other option. I made a bed for her in the living room and went off to my bed. Some time in the night I heard the click of her claws on the polished floor as she left her bed and took up her usual night time position on the mat by my bedroom door. She was obviously feeling much better.

In the morning I was able to phone Larvs at the veterinary department. An hour or so later I saw his dust cloud approaching. He diagnosed kidney trouble and prescribed a course of injections. For the next five days he came each day to give Meg her injections. She made a full recovery. I was most grateful to Larvs.

With the buildings well on schedule and

our slurry pump on site we were well on the way, as the third year started. It was time to try out our new piece of kit. The engineers who had produced it warned me never to let it run dry as there might not be another rubber sleeve in Zambia. I was well used to slurry pumps and fully realised that running the pump dry would overheat the rubber which would distort and soon become useless. For this reason I always had someone in attendance to monitor the pumping and avoid any mishaps. The pump performed well and several weeks passed without incident.

By now the locally purchased gilts, having reared a litter were now either in the dry sow area having been served and gone past the three week return date or were in the service area being attended to. Pondani was the man in charge of those two departments. Each day I collected details of services, the ear tag numbers of the female and the boar used. In my house I had one of those recording wheels which I moved on each day so that a service date eventually moved round until a farrowing date was flagged. It was a system which worked very well but depended on accurate information being supplied by Pondani.

Our daily meetings might go something like this. 'Have the boars been busy today Pondani?'

'Yes Bwana the boars enjoying too much.'

We would then go round collecting ear numbers. Right from our first meeting I had been amused by Pondani's use of the words 'too much' a favourite and much used expression. Pondani had an assistant to help with mucking out and swilling down so often had a few hours of spare time. The arrangement was that he could spend some time pumping slurry but not to leave the pump unattended.

Pondani was on one of these spells of pump duty one day when I paid a visit. As I approached I saw a small figure crouched in the shade of a bush in an attitude which indicated sleep. Smoke poured from the business end of the pump, the pit was pumped dry.

Later, Mahdi questioned Pondani about the incident. 'Was Bwana angry?' he asked.

'Too much,' said Pondani. Perhaps on this occasion he had got it about right. Fortunately spare parts were located and fitted; I doubt if Pondani ever slept on the job again.

★   ★   ★

I still had ideas about having cattle on the place. We had maize stover and sunflower residues and molasses was readily available from the Tate & Lyle sugar cane fields to the south of us. We also had a cattle dip, unused for years but necessary to prevent fly-borne diseases; heart water being the favourite killer. Also there was a functional water trough. All we needed was a stockade to keep the cattle from wandering at night and two youngsters to herd the cattle as they grazed in the bush during the day and at the end of the day to take the cattle to the water trough then to the night quarters to top up on stover and a molasses lick.

As luck would have it the Danish dairy scheme had thirty young cattle they wanted to sell. We had a deal. I diverted some labour to making a stockade and others to clear out the cattle dip which had become overgrown in the bush. Some repair work was needed on cracked rendering but this was soon done and the water bowser came into its own as we tested for leaks. It held water, all was well. Some fencing was needed as a holding pen for cattle about to be dipped. More or less this was sheep dipping on a larger scale.

The cattle arrived. A mixed bunch. Some pretty Zebu humped cattle, Afrikaans with large horns, Brahman and a variety of others which I couldn't put a name to. Two boys eagerly accepted the herding job. Bush grazing topped up by crop residues represented low cost feeding and eventually the young cattle would grow into beef.

For my part I enjoyed seeing the cattle come home at the end of the day, helping the boys to pen them and watching the cattle enjoy the sunflower stover and the molasses lick. I think Meg was happy to see some cattle and, still willing to work, showed a lively interest in guiding the cattle into their pen.

★ ★ ★

The football team had been having a successful season by and large, winning and drawing more than they had lost. I didn't go to all the matches but I always knew if they had won or even drawn when the lorry arrived back packed tight with the team and supporters. A win would be heralded by cheering and singing. This could be heard on the still air a long way off reaching a crescendo as they reached my bungalow and turned off for the compound.

There was one occasion when for some reason John Tembo was not available to drive the lorry. This meant that I had to take on the driving. I had arranged a fixture with a school. I knew it was not too far away but had no idea how to get to it. There seemed to be

197

no shortage of local knowledge and several people offered to direct me.

After all, the guide would get to sit in the cab. We set off. Two people who professed to know the way were in the cab with me. We travelled along the dirt road heading north but soon turned off on to a bush road which seemed to go on and on. I began to doubt my guides. A school in such a remote bush situation? I queried the directions.

'Not far Bwana, go straight.'

I had little option but to go straight and at our fairly low speed it still seemed a long way. At last we arrived. The track led us into a large open space. There was a block built school building, quite large with other buildings which could have been dormitories surrounding a playing field which had a well watered grass surface. The home team were already out, giving their goalkeeper some practice. I soon realised that this was not a team of boys. They looked big and strong, in their late teens or twenties. It brought home to me that starting and leaving ages were arbitrary; a late starter at, say, twelve might leave at eighteen for instance and indeed most schools could produce a proportion of late finishers.

I was greeted warmly by the headmaster, an elderly man, mild mannered and soft spoken. He occupied the only chair on the touchline. He shook hands. 'You are most welcome. But I must get a chair for you.' He beckoned one of the players. 'Please fetch a chair for our guest.'

'You have a wide range of ages,' I said. The old man smiled. 'We have all ages. We teach all we can fit in, to the best of our ability. If someone wants to learn, whatever the age, we do our best to teach them. Football and other sports are important to bond people, make them feel part of a community. We do our best, it is not always easy.'

'Well,' I said, 'let the best team win.' We shook hands on it and settled down to watch as my lads took to the field. I felt so proud of them as they skipped around one of the goals testing the goalkeeper with shots. Such natural athletes, the goalkeeper cat-like in his leaps and pounces, the outfield elegant in their movements, shooting with venom. They had come on a lot since their early days. Peter was not in the team. He was on a week's leave. Tribal custom demanded that he attend a circumcision ceremony at some bush location. I did not enquire as to his functions; he just said he had to assist. I was only thankful that it was boys only, no girls were involved. However we were well placed to give the big lads at the other end a tough game.

At half time we were one down but in the second half Sunday flicked a header towards the top comer and the game finished one each. A very satisfactory result. At the end of the match there were tea and buns, a rare treat and much appreciated. On the way home I joined in the cheering. It had been a hard fought game with a cup final quality about it. Everyone was in high spirits. It would seem only defeat would have dampened the spirits.

20

South Africa

My trip to South Africa was now organised. I had my plane tickets, an allowance of Rand for expenses and I would be met at Jan Smuts airport and provided with a guide for a week. The first snag was that Zambian planes were not flying to South Africa for reasons which were political. I had to take a flight to Blantyre in Malawi and a South African flight from there to Pretoria.

I was met by a member of Fleiscentraal staff who installed me in a hotel. Each morning he collected me and we toured farms in the Pretoria, Johannesburg area. The biggest and perhaps the most progressive of the farmers we met was Mr Brack, of German origin who was able to show us a fine selection of landrace and large white sows and boars and crosses between the two. I purchased one hundred first cross gilts.

At another farm I purchased four landrace boars. A lady farmer who did a lot of showing supplied me with four large white boars and twenty sows. At another farm I picked up twenty landrace sows. I now had enough to set up two pure breeding herds within the total herd and enough boars to provide the crosses. Things would get complicated back at the unit.

We now had a hundred first cross gilts to serve to produce bacon pigs. A number of pure breds to produce more first crosses to produce bacon pigs. Could my lads handle this? Coloured ear tags would help but close supervision would be needed. Of course we had effectively two identical units; this might be used to simplify matters. Pure bred large white one side and landrace the other with criss-crossing between.

With the buying done in four days I had a day to spare. The pigs would be loaded in a railway siding the next day with a two week journey ahead of them. My guide, his name was Andre, still picked me up on my spare day.

'I'll show you a few sights,' he suggested.

'What about a tour of Pretoria,' I said. I had been impressed with what I had seen so far. The town rose up from my hotel to some high point. This was where Andre, an elderly, kindly man took me. We passed some large houses.

'These were the homes of gold millionaires; now I suppose rich business men live there.'

At the top was a fort with a museum, the city spread out below us. Looking over a parapet Andre pointed. 'The Voortrekker monument,' he said. I knew something about the great Voortrekk as Christie Nel's grandparents arrived in Zambia as a result of this historic trek. His grandfather had fallen foul of the dreaded black water fever and died soon after they arrived but the intrepid grandmother created the farm as well as bringing up a family.

Apartheid still held sway and the city was all white in the evening. I asked Andre about this. 'Where do they all go?' I wanted to know.

'I'll show you,' said Andre, 'we have to drive out of town just a little way.'

The first settlement he showed me was mostly a sprawl of wooden huts.

'We can't go in we wouldn't be welcome,' he said.

'Who lives here?'

'Blacks,' Andre answered briefly.

The next township was a little more upmarket. I raised an eyebrow.

'Coloureds,' said Andre.

'They seem to clear the town very efficiently.' I had noticed that after five o'clock there were no black people to be seen.

'Railway,' said Andre, 'direct to the station in their township.'

The seat of Government was on our list.

'One of them,' Andre explained, 'the other one is in Cape Town.'

What impressed me here was the coach loads of children arriving with their teachers to see their Parliament. All the children wore smart uniforms and carried satchels. I couldn't help comparing this evidence of children being educated with the lack of opportunity for the rural children of Zambia.

'A drive round Jo'burg to top it off,' suggested Andre.

Johannesburg seemed to move at a different pace from Pretoria. Traffic was in a hurry and people also seemed to fill the pavements. We drove around for a time, then returned to the more sedate Pretoria.

I had been taken out to dinner one evening by a more senior member of the firm. I guessed he wanted to talk business and the same man and his wife took me to the cinema on my last night. I turned up wearing a shirt and tie and slacks, no jacket. This could probably present a problem, my host informed me. Jackets were normally worn to the cinema. He was several sizes larger than me. I couldn't possibly wear one of his jackets but I could carry it over my arm. Protocol was observed. We saw Straw Dogs.

The next morning found me in the station

yard helping Andre to organise the loading of the pigs. Fleiscentraal were providing pigmen to travel with the pigs as far as the Zambian border. The final part through Zambia they would be unattended but with plenty of food and water to last the final stage of the journey. They arrived in surprisingly good shape. John Tembo and helpers transported them home in relays in the moonlight. They would wake up in the morning comfortably housed in Nkumba pens.

Soon after this, not only did no planes fly between Zambia and South Africa but the border with Rhodesia closed, road blocks sprang up, supplies of fish meal from South Africa could not come through Rhodesia. The demand for soya bean meal increased making for shortages from time to time. We made the best of a bad job, cotton cake was available on occasion, any patches of maize that were not thriving I cut and fed to the nursing sows. We managed. We always managed.

We were about to try our hand at dipping the cattle when Skottke paid a visit.

'You won't like what I have to tell you,' he said.

'That won't stop you telling me,' I said, 'go on, what's the bad news.'

'You are losing Mahdi. He's needed on a farm down near Livingstone. He will have sole charge, a promotion if you like.'

This was a bombshell. I was all for Mahdi moving up to take full responsibility for a farm but I was selfish enough to realise I would miss him. I would miss our table tennis, the odd cricket match which I attended to watch him play and Yasmin made such wonderful curries. Most of all though I would miss his contribution to the farming.

'You will have a replacement,' said Skottke. 'A young Zambian lad. He's bright. I am sure he will soon get the hang of things.'

'Nothing we can do about it' I said, 'when does the blow fall?'

'About a month and that's not all.'

'More bad news?'

'You will have a new line manager in about a month. His name is Roger Miller. He's English. They seem to think I have too much on my plate, I expect it means I will spend more time upstairs at meetings. Come on let me help you dip those cattle. Things will settle down, you'll see.' We set off to plunge the cattle through the dip but my feathers were distinctly ruffled. Mahdi and Samuel were a strong team on the arable side. My new lad would be a learner. I was not happy.

The tractors were getting past their best. Made in Israel they had seen a lot of service. I hoped they would see us through another season. From these brooding thoughts a plan was evolving. Joseph had shown great aptitude for things mechanical, why not get some training laid on for him. I discussed this with the people in Lusaka who normally dealt with our repairs. We agreed in principle that Joseph would work in their workshop, learn what he could from the mechanics, his wages to be paid by Nkumba and his apprenticeship would last for six weeks.

I put the plan to Joseph. He jumped at the opportunity. He could lodge with a relative in Lusaka. Yes he was all for it. So Joseph, already a very good welder was to learn new skills. I wanted him to come back with a knowledge of fault finding, why a tractor wouldn't start, why should one be misfiring or losing power; in other words I wanted him to keep the tractors running. So we would have to manage without Joseph for a time. Who next I wondered. Well there was another. David our most experienced bricklayer announced that he would have to leave for a spell.

'But why, David, are you not happy here?'

'I am happy Bwana but my woman has a problem. She has a dirty disease. I must take her back to Tanzania.'

I could only suppose she had a venereal disease in which case David himself would need some treatment. 'I can take you and your wife to Chelston clinic or to the hospital for treatment.'

'No Bwana I have made up my mind. I will take her back to her people. We will leave in the morning.'

'How long will you be away?'

'Five or six weeks.'

In the morning I watched them leave, David walking ahead; his wife following with a large suitcase on her head.

I had long since learned how these poor people managed to travel vast distances with little money. There was an unofficial transport system in operation. A family would camp on the roadside, perhaps for days until a lorry should come along; there would be some negotiations, then the family would scramble on top of the load and their journey would begin. I often wondered how — without a map or the ability to read one — they knew where they were going. I suppose the lorry driver would have some responsibility to take them in the right direction. I hoped the twenty Kwacha I slipped in David's pocket would smooth their passage.

'It's a bonus David for all your good work, I hope you will come back.'

I was left to marvel at the hardiness that enabled those with so little money to undertake the uncertainties and hardship of this mode of travel.

★ ★ ★

Mahdi and Yasmin left for their new farm, Yasmin now heavily pregnant. I promised to come on a visit once the baby was born. Joseph was already in Lusaka and reported to be popular and doing well. Our new line manager had been out to see what went on at Nkumba. He was a pleasant man a bit younger than me and seemed happy enough for me to keep him informed and he was there if I wanted to discuss anything. He was also not at all bad at table tennis. My new assistant would be with me in the next few days and Renee would soon be out for a short holiday. John and Trish would not visit. John was off to Bristol to study for the Auctioneers and Valuers qualification. Trish had her sights on a Hotel Management and Catering course at Norwich City College. This would mean Renee selling up our Devon home and buying something in Norwich. My next leave would no doubt be to our new home in Norwich. But we were not done with comings and goings. Lamek had something to tell me. 'Positani wants my girl Losta, I think it's OK.'

I was shocked. 'But she's still a child. You

can't do this Lamek. She is too young.'

'She is nearly fifteen Bwana. Soon she is a woman. Positani is OK. Losta will move to the compound. That is good. Not far.'

'Has Positani enough money?' Positani was a useful bricklayer.

'He gave me forty kwachas. This is good, everybody pays forty kwacha.'

There was little I could do. This was custom, not to be denied. It saddened me though when I thought of Losta, still a child, small, thin, immature; child bearing would start all too soon, she would carry water, cook the mealie porridge, nurse her children, her own childhood finished far too soon.

And so it happened. A week later Losta left for the compound. She carried a small bundle on her head. Lamek would have been paid. Forty kwachas was two months wages, twenty pounds in U.K. money. This might have been the end of the matter but it was not to be. About two months later a troubled Lamek approached me. I could tell at once that he was downcast; there was no smile, he seemed listless.

'Are you not well Lamek?' I asked, 'or do you have problems?'

'I need to have day off tomorrow Bwana.'

'Of course Lamek, but tell me what is troubling you, perhaps I can help.'

'I must go to witch doctor tomorrow.'

I waited, there was more to come.

'Positani has brought Losta back. He says she is not satisfactory. He wants his money back. Is tomorrow OK.?'

'Of course Lamek. But can the witch doctor help?'

'He will tell me what to do.'

'Then you must go tomorrow.'

As the sun came up the next morning I saw Lamek set off followed by his wife and children. They were gone most of the day. The following morning Lamek reported for work looking more like his usual cheerful self.

'So what happened?'

Lamek stood for a moment gathering his thoughts then with a broad smile on his face he said. 'It was good Bwana, everything is now OK.'

'I want to know what happened. You must tell me everything.'

'The witchdoctor listened to our problem then he gave me a piece of paper. There is nothing on the paper. He holds it to the fire, some writing comes on the paper. He reads it. It is a curse on Positani. If he makes trouble the curse will make him ill.'

I understood about the invisible ink, how the rest of it should work I never understood but Positani remained in perfect health; as far as I knew Lamek kept the money and Losta settled back into the family to resume her childhood. Hocus-pocus maybe but it seemed to have worked.

★　★　★

With Renee on a visit it seemed like a good idea to check up on Mahdi and Yasmin. I had heard that they now had a baby girl. We set off having arranged to spend the weekend with them. It was the usual long haul down to Livingstone, interrupted at intervals by road blocks and a search of the car. Renee was less than happy about pointed rifles and the searching which included lifting the bonnet — what did they expect to find — and peering at our luggage. I had come to accept this as a way of life, distasteful though it was. Having made a fuss of the baby and discussed the farming we were informed that another couple would be staying. This did not present any problems as they had a large farmhouse. There was to be a tennis tournament on the next day.

The other couple arrived; a Scottish girl and a turbaned Sikh. He was short and rather squat, middle-aged, she would be in her thirties, an ill assorted couple. During the evening they would suddenly get up and go outside for perhaps twenty minutes. This struck us as odd as they didn't make any explanation, no — 'we are just going out for a breath of fresh air', just a sudden, abrupt exit. Discussing this odd behaviour later Renee and I decided they were going out for a smoke, probably cannabis.

Yasmin cooked one of her really hot curries which I enjoyed. Renee at the time was nursing a gall bladder problem and was on a white fish diet. I suppose she did have reason to complain about my breath that night.

We attended the tennis tournament on the Sunday. Mahdi was not the star at tennis that he was at table tennis and cricket. Mahdi and Yasmin seemed settled in their new home; they had a fine baby, a good house and Mahdi seemed to be on top of the work. All was well, we set off on the long journey back. The road blocks were still in place.

21

A Shooting

We had a tearful, disturbing phone call from Diane Nel. She was agitated and having difficulty getting the words out.

'What is it Diane? Are you in some sort of trouble?' Her next words were a hammer blow.

'Christie's been shot,' she said.

'Not . . . ?'

'No, he's not dead, but badly wounded. He's in the hospital in Lusaka.'

'But how? Diane, tell me what happened.'

Calmer now, Diane explained. 'He went to look for elephants with Tom. You know Tom?'

Yes I knew who she was talking about.

'Well they got down near the border and were driving along a track when they were ambushed by freedom fighters. They were firing bullets all round the Land Rover. Christie and Tom had to stop. They were then captured and taken to a camp in the bush.'

This was about all Diane knew. 'We'll be at the hospital by first light, I said. 'Call us for any help you need.'

By six the next morning we were at the hospital. An armed policeman sat on guard outside Christie's room. We were allowed to go in. Christie was propped up, coughing. A nurse was patting his back and had an arm round him for support. Christie's spasm passed and he saw us standing by the bed.

'The bastards tortured me,' he said pointing to burn marks where his beard had been, 'and I still have a bullet in my guts.' The nurse took us aside. 'He needs to rest, don't overtire him. They didn't remove the bullet, it has lodged near his liver. There is no immediate danger; the bullet can be removed later.'

'He seems to need to cough, should we call you if it starts up again?'

'There is a lot of phlegm on his lungs which he needs to cough up. Just prop him up and support him. I won't be far away.'

Christie seemed to want to talk. He pointed again to his chin.

'Yes I see they have burned off your nice little Jan Smuts beard,' I said.

'With burning brands from the fire. I couldn't do a thing. Too many holding me down. Drunk, out of their heads. Next time I want my beard off I'll go to the barbers.'

A fit of coughing consumed him. We propped him up and held a receptacle. The

215

nurse popped her head in. 'All right?'

'Yes fine, he's doing well.'

'That nurse hardly leaves me. She might as well get in bed with me.' He tried to smile. His eyes closed. He looked very tired. After a few minutes his eyes opened.

'I must tell you how it was. The short version. Later on man when I'm better I can go on a bit.'

'The short version will do well,' I said.

'Well, here goes. They stopped our vehicle with bullets. We were captured, hands tied. One got behind the wheel; the others piled in the back. We were taken to their camp in the bush. I was kept there but Tom was taken to some other camp. They said I was a spy and did the torture bit.'

Renee was outraged. 'But you were born here, you are as Zambian as they are.'

'I have a Zambian passport and I have a South African one, it made no odds to them, they were drunk and wanted some sport.' Another bout of coughing interrupted the narrative.

'Perhaps you should rest,' I suggested.

'No, no I must tell you.'

'OK. what next?'

'They stood me up and started shooting round my feet. They were shouting, 'Dance, dance.''

'I wouldn't dance; then a bullet ricocheted off a stone. That's the one in my guts. I can't describe the pain I was in.' At this point Christie's eyes closed again.

'Perhaps we should go, we may be tiring him,' Renee whispered.

Christie's eyes opened. 'No don't go, there is not much to tell. Just remind me where I had got to.'

'The bullet, the awful pain. Surely they looked after you then.'

'Not until an officer chanced upon the scene. Even then he took me to the police station in Lusaka where he told them his men thought I was a spy. The sods questioned me. I was out of my mind with pain. It was the police who brought me here after they were sure I was a local farmer on a legitimate hunting trip.'

'They still left a fat policeman outside your door,' I said.

'Just show, to justify the shooting,' Christie chuckled then held his abdomen, laughing would be painful for some time. 'My nurse, she's very much on my side. She says she won't be offering my guard any breakfast and if he leaves his post she will report him. She's fairly steamed up about the shooting.'

'Well just make sure she doesn't get into bed with you; we would have to tell Diane.' I said, 'now we must leave you to rest.'

Later we discovered that Tom had been held overnight then allowed to drive home in his vehicle. He was shaken by the experience but undamaged. A few weeks later there was a short item in the Times of Zambia which reported that Christie Nel, a local farmer had been involved in a shooting accident while hunting in the bush.

It was almost a year later that Christie went south to have the bullet removed in a South African hospital.

22

Dog Bite

I had always felt there was a jinx operating whenever Renee was on holiday. Her holiday was nearly over, perhaps this time nothing untoward would happen. No such luck, this time was to be no exception. We had been driving in the bush for some time, Renee was behind the wheel. I was well aware that it is easy enough to lose your sense of direction in such a featureless place so, although my bush credentials were much improved we stayed on well used paths. All went well until we came upon a hollow with some standing water.

'Give it some wellie,' was my advice. The momentum would surely carry us through. Unfortunately Renee did not fancy a splash through and took her foot off the accelerator. The result was that we were stuck in the middle with some wheel spin and no forward movement. We got out to survey our predicament and then a strange thing happened. In a place deep in the bush apparently uninhabited by any human form, a man appeared. He carried a spear and was followed by a nondescript pack of dogs.

I recognised this man as our recently appointed night watchman who had taken over from the original young man who had tired of night duties. The man now offering his help obviously used his daylight hours to go hunting in the bush. I elected to drive, hoping to creep the car out of the wet hole. With Renee and the man pushing behind, the pick-up started to move. It was during the inevitable shouting of instructions and encouragement that one of the dogs, joining in the fun, bit Renee on the leg. Rabies immediately came to mind; this bite could not be taken lightly; a trip to hospital was indicated; I turned the pick-up, and skirting the wet hole we set off the way we had come.

At the hospital we joined others seated round a room. The doctor was working his way round the patients, consulting, listening to symptoms, sometimes giving injections where they sat, sometimes taking a patient into his room for more detailed examination. Next to us sat two children suffering from veld sores; large nasty looking holes deep into their legs. Eventually it was Renee's turn. She related events in detail. The doctor took us into his room to clean and put a plaster on the punctures.

He said. 'I think it is unlikely that this dog

was rabid. It sounds like an excitable dog reacting to a situation. The rabies injections are unpleasant. I propose to give you an antibiotic but do keep an eye on the dog for any unusual behaviour.' He duly administered a large dose of penicillin. The next day Renee had ballooned, face, hands, fingers like sausages. It was then that we discovered for the first time that she was allergic to penicillin. An Indian doctor in Lusaka put her on antihistamine and she soon returned to normal.

A few days later, her holiday over, she flew home. It was then that I thought about the dog. I knew which one it was, small, and the only black one in the pack. It was missing — my heart missed a beat.

'Where is the black dog?' I asked.

'Black dog dead, Bwana; killed by pig.'

While this was quite possible — a bush pig defending its young could be formidable I wanted to hear more but the man's English was very limited. I had Samuel speak to him. Samuel reported a little more fully. A wild pig had defended her litter successfully against the pack but the black dog got too close and was killed.

'But,' Samuel said, 'Chinyanja was not his best language. He speaks Swahili.

Well, Mahdi spoke fluent Swahili. We had

the night watchman in my house for several mornings to be cross-examined by Mahdi. The night watchman stuck to his version of events.

Somewhat mollified I went about my business with an easier mind, that is until some weeks later. Visiting a convalescing Christie, I picked up a magazine, which carried an article on rabies. The line that jumped out at me stated, rabies could appear up to nine months after the initial infection. So started a period of anxiety. Reports from home continued to be good and my worries eased somewhat. Then I had a letter in which Renee said she was suffering from a cold; her throat was sore and she was so thirsty. Thirsty — hydrophobia? The worry stepped up a gear, then she was fine again and so it went on. Time passed and all was well. Had the jinx struck again? One had to wonder.

I was finally completely happy when I had my next leave. We had moved to Norwich in the meantime. I was met at the station by our now seventeen year old daughter. 'Car's outside Dad. Passed first time.'

'You're going to drive me home in all this traffic? By the way how's your Mum?'

'Waiting to have an op, gall bladder, but she's fine. Come on, it's the rush hour, let's get you home.'

⋆   ⋆   ⋆

It was following Renee's dog bite incident that I had a chat with Larvs. I had become very aware that we lived in a rabies country. 'What about getting some of the dogs vaccinated,' I asked.

'Your Meg would be done when you arrived?'

'Yes complying with the law, but I doubt if any others are done.'

'We'll fix a day,' said Larvs, 'Spread the word and I will come with plenty of vaccine.'

We agreed a day, I spread the word, relying on the bush telegraph to do the rest. I woke up on the appointed day and couldn't believe what I was seeing. The sun was barely over the horizon, my lawn was full of men and dogs, single dogs, small packs, all shapes and sizes, Some tied to my trees and bushes, Some men standing, some reclining. I hoped Larvs would bring enough vaccine. The word had gone far and wide.

Larvs arrived. We set up a table. The dogs came past in turn. Larvs injected, I wrote certificates. The vaccine held out. Everyone was happy. Lamek made a pot of tea. I had my lawn back.

23

Lusaka Show

My new arable assistant was now settled in. Like many young Africans he had adopted an English name, Paul. A tall well set up young man, with a good head on his shoulders. He had his own car, a confident approach to his responsibilities and with Samuel behind him I was sure he would handle the arable side with minimal input from me. To give him an area where he would be in full charge I gave him the cattle to supervise. This delighted him. He was very much a cattle person and could be seen most evenings walking among the herd doing a careful inspection. Heart water was the term commonly used to describe a fly borne infection which inevitably resulted in the death of the animal. Dipping helped to control this pest but was not a guarantee that the odd beast would not go down with it.

It was one evening when the cattle were grazing a grassy area not far from their night corral that one went down. Paul was soon on my doorstep. 'One is dying, heart water, Bwana. I think there is not much we can do.'

I went with him to inspect the ailing animal. It was a pretty little Zebu heifer, obviously very ill. She lay flat out, eyes dilated, breathing laboured. I had never seen heart water so was in no position to judge. On the other hand it went against the grain not to try to help the suffering animal.

'We must try to help her,' I said.

'But how Bwana. Heart water kills.'

'You wait here, I will be back soon.' I went back to my house, found a large bottle and had a rummage through a collection of pig remedies. There were quite a few soluble medicines which were designed to add to drinking water. I proceeded to mix a cocktail of these. I could only guess on quantities but erred if anything on the generous side. Back with the sick animal I held up the bottle. 'I am now going to show you how to bottle an animal without choking it.' This I proceeded to do.

'What do we do now Bwana?'

'Cover her with sacks to keep her warm. Let me know how she is in the morning.'

I had just finished calling the register in the morning when Paul arrived miming and looking rather excited. 'Bwana, Bwana, she is better, on her feet and eating grass.'

I could hardly believe it. My ministrations the night before had been more to salve my

225

own conscience, to feel that I had done something; I never expected this positive result. Just as excited as Paul I went with him to behold this miracle. True enough the little heifer was grazing happily with the others and indeed she never looked back. My young assistant looked at me in awe. Here was a man who could cure heart water.

Paul said. 'You tell me about the medicine.'

'Of course,' I said 'realising that this would be difficult as my concoction was of the hit or miss variety or perhaps it was more kill or cure.' I hoped we didn't get another case which might be incurable heart water. My reputation was made as far as Paul was concerned, he would expect a miracle every time.

Paul, as I mentioned had his own car, Peter Mwema had a company issue motor bike. This was a rather flashy Honda with twin upswept exhausts. There was an occasion when my car was in for a service and pulling rank I commandeered Peter's motorbike. Motorbikes had been a feature of my youth and I was rather enjoying my trips to and from the site. When Paul saw me dirt tracking on the dusty road he was horrified. 'Bwana, Bwana' he cried. 'You mustn't, you must have my car, you are *mandala*, the old one, the wise one.'

I wasn't too keen on the 'old one' but 'the wise one' had a ring to it. When I was home and told my wife that I was regarded as the wise one — I chose not to mention the old one bit — and was known to perform the odd miracle, she said rather drily, 'I have a list of things you could be getting on with here.' Women have a way of keeping your feet on the ground.

★　★　★

With Lusaka Show in the offing I decided we could afford the luxury of showing a few pigs. I had also been asked to provide a Nkumba exhibit. Preparation of the show pigs had to start. The selected pigs were housed, together with reserves, apart from the other pigs. I sought to improve their diet and someone told me that the dairy which imported Australian milk powder sometimes had broken bags to dispose of. I availed myself of some and soon the show pigs had the bloom of thriving, well nourished pigs. A few weeks before the show I applied a mild blister of pig oil and flowers of sulphur, a skin improver which also got rid of any coarse hair. They were looking well, and, being walked and handled, soon became friendly and manageable.

Next I had to turn my mind to the show stand. I thought a sow and litter might fill the bill housed in a comfortable pen, with an outside area and a rear sleeping section. I had in mind that the occupants had to be seen even when resting so the house had to be fairly open. The outer pen would be enclosed by a fence of wooden slats with a one inch gap between. The sleeping area would have plywood walls to waist height the whole being covered by an elephant grass thatch.

I had a sow rearing twelve which would be well grown on the day. The sow was on show rations and the piglets would soon be creep feeding. Sunday and a team went off to the showground each day in the lorry with tools and timber for the framework. I checked progress each day to make sure uprights were plumb and cross pieces level. We would be in the public eye, this was our showpiece.

I had thatched ricks in my early days. I wanted a tidy job. Christie Nel showed me how to turn elephant grass which has a strong flag into good looking thatch. A stand was made to about waist high, this supported a sloping board through which nails had been driven with the sharp points facing upwards. Handfuls of the elephant grass is drawn through the bed of nails till all the flag is removed. Time consuming, but strong straight thatch results. The thatch when laid and tied down with string and the edges clipped looked great.

I was immensely proud of our exhibit, especially when the sow, in show condition with twelve eight week old piglets for company and deeply bedded in maize stover, took up residence on the morning of the show. Other exhibits had to be attended on the Show morning. All were shampooed and dried off with wood flour. All were in prime condition.

The fact that we swept the board in all the classes we had entered had something to do with our presentation and a lot to do with the poor quality of the opposition. A pair of baconers won their class as did a pair of maiden gilts. Our sow won her class and got Best in Show. The boar won his class and was runner up to the sow in the championship. Nkumba had acquitted itself well.

Of course, unlike a show back home nobody had to worry about the weather, everything took place in brilliant sunshine. Our fine thatch was a sunshade and never had to deflect a drop of rain. There was much cheering back at the unit when the rosettes were displayed.

24

Sister Jo

Soon another harvest was upon us. I began to realize that my contract would be over in a few months. I took stock of where we were in terms of buildings, pigs and arable. The buildings would all be finished, I was confident that we would complete on time, also that I could keep all the workforce employed to the end. I worried a bit about what would happen to the many workers when Nkumba construction side closed down. Pigs, if we counted in the maiden gilts would be up to five hundred breeding and potential breeding animals. The cattle could carry on until someone decided they were saleable. Arable farming would proceed as at present. I did not intend to stay on so a new manager would have to be appointed. I had heard whispers that a new contract would be offered to me soon but I felt my work was done, I wanted to go home to my family.

Meantime the combine was eating up the crop at a spectacular rate. Both maize and sunflower seemed to be yielding reasonably well. I had persuaded Lamek to plant up his little bit of land with maize and this he had done. Lamek was pleased with his small crop of maize; I was pleased with two banana plants which Iron had told me would produce fruit provided I gave them plenty of water. This I did religiously, carrying buckets of water each evening and finally seeing small bananas forming. I watched these dangling trusses, waiting impatiently for the fruit to become part of my food supply.

Well, the best laid schemes . . . I was destined never to sample my carefully tended fruit and it was all down to Lamek. Lamek had handpicked his small patch of maize and prudently, to tidy up his patch, to keep it free from lurking snakes or encroaching bush fire he had decided to burn off the stubble and crop residues. Unfortunately he had not taken enough care to prevent the fire encroaching into my garden. The bananas were at the end of my garden close to Lamek's patch. They bore the brunt of it before the fire petered out on the cultivated part of the garden. This was the only time I had reason to be angry with Lamek who looked after my every need so diligently. Lamek bore my anger stoically. The next day it was all behind us. As always in this country whatever the tragedy, big or small, tomorrow was a new dawn.

★ ★ ★

I soon got things into perspective when one of the labourers approached me and told me he had a sick child. 'Very sick Bwana crying all the time. It is not good.'

'Then we must get him into hospital right away. I will bring the pick-up to your Nyumba and we will leave now now.' I had learned enough of the language to know that repetition indicated urgency.

'No Bwana, no hospital. I must go to the witch doctor. I need the day off.'

'No,' I said to him. 'No witch doctor I must get this child into hospital, the sooner the better.'

'No Bwana, no hospital.'

'But why?'

'I have one child get sick. Go to hospital and die in hospital. No more hospital.'

It was a familiar story. So often when a child finally was taken to hospital it would be too late, the child was already dying. I could see I would not win this argument. 'OK. Take the day off. I wish you luck.'

He was gone most of the day. It was late afternoon when he returned. He came to see me. 'Witch doctor says he cannot help my child. I must take him to the hospital.'

I was much concerned that we were already

too late. The witch doctor probably had enough medical knowledge to recognise a dying child. And so it proved, my next request was to collect the child's body from the mortuary. We set off, the father seated beside me, impassive, with little to say.

At the mortuary I pulled up at the door. 'Go inside and find your child, I will wait here.'

Time passed and finally he came out empty handed. 'Bwana there is no-one to help me and I cannot read.'

So, there was no attendant, we were obviously expected to help ourselves. I went along the labelled drawers reading the names. 'This is your child.' I said sadly. I pulled the drawer open. Inside was a brown paper parcel. We collected his child and he cradled the pathetic little parcel as we drove off. On the way home we passed a dead Kululu on the roadside. 'Stop Bwana I get it.'

He had a dead child on his lap but back at the Nyumba he had a live family to feed. He ran back down the road and came back carrying the kululu. 'Nyama,' (meat) he said. He didn't speak again until we were back at the farm. All he said was, 'box Bwana.'

'Yes,' I said 'I will make you a nice box.'

I delivered the box the next day. The child was buried in the bush. There was nothing to mark the grave. There was some drinking in the evening and in the morning the young father returned to work. The episode was finished. As I said earlier, each day brought a new dawn.

★ ★ ★

It was just before the Lusaka Show that my line manager Roger Miller had a bad car accident and facing a long convalescence he departed for Australia. His wife was Australian and I presume Roger would be nursed back to fitness in the care of his wife and her family. There had been a delay in appointing a new man but now a new name had been added to the senior management team. His surname was Richelieu — yes the same as the infamous Cardinal — and he was Danish. Of course with our project so well advanced and within budget we had little need for contact with head office so we saw our new line manager infrequently. He was perhaps in his late fifties or early sixties and seemed to settle in quite quickly. He seemed happy enough to let us plod on at Nkumba and he did not have the opportunity that Skottke had, to become involved.

Another new face came within my orbit about this time. Sister Jo was a nun who was engaged in training local girls in the ways of the Christian faith on an agricultural holding which I knew existed on the way to Lusaka. I had seen white-robed figures working in their vegetable plots some way off the road as I drove past. I had no more knowledge of this enterprise until Sister Jo arrived with some of her trainees in a Land Rover. It seemed that they would like to start up a small pig enterprise. The pigs could use up crop residues and add importantly to the turnover of their business.

I was happy to show them round and explain what we were doing. Yes they could purchase a few gilts from us and I would contribute where I could with help and advice. I invited Sister Jo to come round one afternoon, so that we could discuss this further over a cup of coffee. I was curious about Sister Jo and her community of nuns. She was a bright cheerful little woman approaching middle age, full of enthusiasm for her work and with a lively sense of humour.

About two weeks later she turned up again. Over coffee, with discreet questioning I learned about her past history. I knew of course that she was American, her accent gave that away. I never did learn why she became a nun but when she did, there had been no half measures. She entered a closed order where she stayed for over twenty years shut away from the world and her family, friends or outside contacts. How she moved from this to her present state I never discovered but she seemed not to be harmed in any way by her long incarceration.

It was during this visit that she spotted the table tennis set up. 'Ping Pong what fun. I used to play in my young days.'

'Would you like a game?' I suggested rather hesitantly. I had not played recently. Richelieu didn't play and in any case had only been out a couple of times. Skottke had less reason to call now though he did look in once in a while, Mahdi my regular opponent was three hundred miles away. 'I need the practice,' I went on.

'I haven't played for years but I would love a game.'

She was not a bad performer and I shall never forget the small figure bouncing and leaping, her voluminous black habit flapping and the sweat beading on her forehead. We played again a few weeks later and arranged for the sale of four in-pig gilts to the convent. She called on other occasions, sometimes in need of advice but always played table tennis which she played with vigour and enthusiasm. These sessions usually ended with a look at the watch and a hurried departure and a remark like, 'I must go. Can't be late for prayers.'

She had explained that her work consisted of a mix of field work and prayers five times a day. I often wondered how many times she was late for prayers.

25

Sports Day

The time had come to consider the end of my contract. In a few short weeks I would be heading for home. I had to decide what I was going to do about my dog Meg. I could not subject her to six months in quarantine which she would never survive in any case. I would have to steel myself to arrange for her to be put down. I made a box, I was well practised at making boxes by now and took it along to Larvs who now lived in a house not far from Skottke in Blue Boar Road. 'This is for Meg. I would like to leave her with you when I leave. When I'm out of the country I want you to do the necessary including burial.' Larvs agreed and this is how we left it. I heard much later that he had kept Meg living with him till his contract was up.

Another thing on my mind was the imminent unemployment facing people on the building side of things. About all I could do was to give each man a reference, detailing the work he was doing and his level of skill if this applied or his ability to work hard as a labourer. I would give some thought to each note I wrote and these would be handed out on the last pay day. I hoped the skills learned by a number of the men would not be wasted.

Another concern was how I should mark my departure. I could pack my case and just slip away but I felt I owed the community more than that. A party of some sort, but what? Then it struck me. A sports day would be a day for all to enjoy either as competitors or as spectators. My mind started to race through the programme, but first I had to go to the police for permission to hold such an event. Any gathering of people had to have a permit from the police so my first task was to arrange a meeting with the most senior policeman in the Lusaka police station. This I did and had a short interview with a smiling pleasant man. I explained the purpose of my gathering and discussed the proposed pro-gramme with him. He readily gave me a permit but with the proviso that I should invite the local police to attend.

The first hurdle over I settled down to some serious planning. The sports field would be prepared, a running track would be graded to encircle the football field, the workshop would cater for high jump stands and bar, a long jump pit would be dug and filled with sand and last but by no means least a refreshment bar would be erected on the touchline. I gave this last item some thought. No chibuku would be served until late afternoon. The bar itself I wanted to look like a bar; thatched with Elephant grass, front clad to bar height, a wide shelf for serving the drinks, partly clad on the other sides with an entrance from the back. This, I thought, could serve as a changing room or other function for the football team.

The stage was set. I enlisted the help of Stuart McGee and his wife Jill to help on the day. It was Mrs McGee who suggested some coloured sweet drinks for the children and a stack of bread to go with it.

Invitations went out to my friends and colleagues and word was being spread on the bush telegraph to people outside Nkumba. There would be no shortage of spectators — or drinkers. I asked Samuel to supervise the production of plenty of chibuku. Other drinks I had stored at my house. As an afterthought I had some wood collected for a giant bonfire to light up proceedings after nightfall. I was as prepared as I could be, now for the event.

On the day people began to line the touchline soon after first light. Where had they all come from? How far had they walked? I had given out that the sports would start at ten. Of course they would not have wrist watches to consult, sunrise and sunset were enough, the in-between did not count for much. I had been impressed on the site when I called a halt to work at two in the afternoon to notice that a stake was being driven in to mark where the shadow fell. A primitive sundial, no less. The crowd would swell before ten o'clock, it was a heartening response. I had a goodly list of entrants for the various events, I had a loud hailer, borrowed from one of the government departments and the bonfire had risen to spectacular dimensions. Always aware of health and safety I made sure the fire would not present a hazard. A photographer friend who had agreed to come and record the event had fallen foul of the authorities in some way and did not turn up. There was a police presence hovering near the bar. The stage was set.

The fun began at ten with a cycle race. Unfortunately there were only two bikes on the farm. Both were in the category of old bangers but functioned. One of the competitors had cut his jacket into strips so that as he tore round the track his mutilated jacket flowed behind in his slip stream. The race was four laps and recklessly ridden but both finished. The torn jacket was the winner by a yard or so. I thought his showmanship deserved a reward. There was a first and second prize so each received a money prize.

High jump followed with Sunday winning with style and grace and so it went on through the programme which included children's races, novelty races and a three legged race for the ladies all enthusiastically received by the spectators and working up to the football. My lads in their yellow T-shirts were up against a team led by McGee consisting of company employees, friends, project managers and anyone who was prepared to brave the heat of the afternoon and take part. I refereed and was delighted to see Nkumba lads moving the ball about, conserving their energy and putting away six goals without reply.

I could sense that people were getting thirsty not least the local police so after checking that the barmen were in place and the chibuku ready I signalled that the bar was open. It seemed that everyone had brought a drinking receptacle, mostly tin cans of reasonable size so service was a quick dip in the chibuku drum and another satisfied customer left the bar. The children likewise were formed up in an orderly line to receive their bottles of pop and a slice of bread. They were very happy with this and soon were off playing their own games probably thinking that pop tasted better than water.

A group of ladies lined up. I was informed that they had a song which they had put together for my departure. They sang, swaying slightly with the rhythm of the song. They were singing in Chinyanja, but it was smooth and pleasant to the ear. The only thing I recognised was the refrain which was in English. It was, 'Bye Bye Tomasoni.'

I was deeply touched by this and thanked them in the African way, one hand held in front of the body, the other held above it, an up and down clap or two accompanied by a bobbing of the knees.

As we approached the onset of evening, preparations were being made to light the bonfire. A small boy surrounded by a circle of ladies demonstrated a dance which looked to me like some fertility routine. Drums were being arranged. A witch doctor in full regalia emerged from the bush, his entrance losing some impact when soon after he was out in the open he fell into an ant-bear hole. He dusted himself down and came among us; I had little difficulty recognising Positani from the building site. Obviously he was not the real thing but I appreciated the effort he must have put in to acquire the fancy dress and make an entrance.

The bonfire was lit as darkness fell and blazed skywards to cheers from the now convivial drinkers. It was time for me and my friends to repair to my house. The party would go on all night as long as the chibuku held out. I had strung lights along the front of my house so that we could make use of the lawn. I have to report that some of my party celebrated rather too well but all got home safely.

Christie Nel had supplied some folding chairs which had been housed in one of his outhouses. These apparently harboured a creature which locals referred to as the Putsi fly. I had been sitting in one of the chairs and it would seem that one of these flies had taken the opportunity to find a home for its eggs under my skin in much the same way as the warble fly, well known to farmers in Britain, and the result was much the same, maggots erupting through the skin. I was back home when this happened much to my horror. I had not fully understood the life cycle of the Putsi fly before but now I understood why Lamek ironed all the clothes from the washing line including my under-pants. 'Flies lay bad things,' he had said when I queried this. I should have listened. I had brought home more than my souvenirs.

Our son and daughter-in-law were staying with us in Norwich at the time. She was an experienced and senior nurse. She managed to extract one maggot from behind my knee, but one that was burrowing in my bottom proved more elusive. She declared that we would have to go to hospital.

We duly went to the Accident and Emergency Department of the local hospital. I was in a cubicle, awaiting someone to attend to me when there was a change of shift. I heard a member of staff saying to the nurse coming on duty. 'This one has a maggot in his bottom and the doctor says we may have to cut the section out.' However, with some difficulty the creature was extracted, but I had to return a few times to have the wound dressed. I discovered afterwards that the simple cure was to pour oil into the site and the maggot would come out itself.

Post Script

In 1978 I paid a visit to Zambia to see how Nkumba was progressing. I stayed with the Nels. The Nkumba project had at last been Zambianised with a Zambian piggery manager and a Zambian Arable manager. Christie took me to visit Nkumba one afternoon. The two managers greeted us enthusiastically, treating us like honoured guests.

The arable staff were unchanged with Samuel still their Capitaal and with Joseph now doing tractor repairs and general maintenance. At the piggery Pondani stepped forward bobbing his knees and clapping his hands one above the other. I responded in kind and followed up with a handshake.

'Maoka bwangi Bwana' he said.

'Taoka,' I replied, 'kodi malipo?'

'I am well,' he replied, returning the conversation to English, and adding after a pause, 'too much.'

'Do you remember the day you fell asleep and ruined the slurry pump?' Pondani's grin widened, then he began to laugh. Soon he was laughing uncontrollably. Others who had gathered round, many of whom I recognised as old hands joined in. The incident had clearly been related round many evening cook-fires. The laughter was infectious, I began to chuckle also. I was remembering the recriminations I had heaped upon Pondani and his reply when I accused him of sleeping on the job.

'Too much Bwana,' he had said.

Just for once his well used phrase had fitted the occasion.

The piggery looked cared for and tidy. Pens were well stocked; the lawns had flourished and bougainvillea which had sprouted in my time now cascaded over buildings. The building staff including Sunday had moved on. Peter Mwema we learned had a period of being very political and had raised a flagpole to fly the UNIP flag. He apparently did not last long at Nkumba. His whereabouts were not known. My other young Zambian assistant who had replaced Mahdi had also moved on. Mahdi and Yasmin were still down at Livingstone.

The Skottke family had left Zambia soon after my departure. Martin worked in Bonn for a few years but the lure of Africa was too strong; he returned to work in Benin and finally in Malawi. Most of my fellow project managers had finished their contracts and moved on. Christie Nel had gone in for extensive fencing and was ranching some cattle with a lucrative contract to supply the Zambian army. Larvs had returned to Denmark where I visited him some years later. He had set up a one man veterinary practice in a village, had acquired some land and was breeding beef cattle. Ben Van Kuringen had moved to South Africa.

The day after our visit to Nkumba I noticed Christie busy around his Land Rover. There was a drum of water on board and various supplies and blankets were being loaded as well as what looked like two camp beds.

'What's on Christie?' I asked.

'We are going hunting man. You've never spent time in the bush, sleeping under the stars, hearing the night noises as the predators get about.'

'I've managed all right so far without all that,' I said and indeed I had steadfastly refused to accompany him on his annual forays. I was not a hunter. I had no wish to kill a fine animal for no good reason.

'I won't expect you to shoot anything man, just keep me company. It will be an experience you will never forget.' I could see Christie had made up his mind. I was his guest; I could hardly refuse. Anyway I would enjoy spending time in the bush. The prospect was exciting. After a substantial breakfast we were on our way. Two of Christie's workers crouched among the baggage behind.

'It's three hundred miles to a free hunting area. I have a licence for a roan antelope. It's a head I haven't got.'

My sympathies were with the Roan antelope but the rest of it seemed like a great adventure. We bowled along three hundred miles of mostly tarred road but finally turned off down a bush track. I had seen this track on the map, a straight line which went on for hundreds of miles bisecting the bush east to west. About thirty miles down this track Christie turned off into the bush. He had spotted a place to establish our camp.

Christie and his two helpers soon had the camp organised. The two camp beds were unloaded. I waited for the tents but they didn't appear.

'Best park your bed under a tree,' Christie advised me, 'it will keep the dew off you in the morning.' When he had mentioned sleeping under the stars he had meant it litcrally.

That night I heard a lion roar. It was some distance away which was comforting but I thrilled to the sound. It was majestic, a free lion in its own habitat announcing its presence.

As night fell we sat on folding chairs by a large campfire and chatted, but we were tired, it was soon time for bed. There was a definite chill in the air. I was glad that I had tossed my suitcase with my cold weather clothes still inside into the back of the Land Rover. I was wearing a light weight safari suit with shorts and sandals. For bed I pulled on extra underwear, a shirt, socks, long casual trousers and a sweater.

With a blanket covering me completely including my head I was very comfortable. Sometime in the night I woke to the sound of digging. Christie was over by the fire digging out a hollow in the ground.

'Digging a grave?' I enquired.

'I'm bloody cold,' the intrepid hunter admitted. The cold comes up through the camp bed. I'm going to try lying on the ground in this hollow.'

'Goodnight,' I said 'don't forget to set the alarm.'

Each day we drove off to look for a Roan antelope. One worker was left behind to collect firewood, do some cooking and have hot water ready for our evening ablutions. The other man stood in the back to spot our target Roan antelope. Navigation was simple. The track ran east to west. If we drove west along the track in the morning then turned right into the bush heading north we were guided back to the track by the position of the setting sun. A left turn on to the track and carry on till we spotted our camp.

After a wash and some food we would have a nip of whisky and discuss the lack of success so far. Christie rather ungraciously accepted a share of my U.K. clothes and our nights passed peacefully apart from an invasion of red ants which Christie repelled with a ring of hot ash and burning brands to discourage further incursions.

On another night it was reported that an old lion had passed by. It had taken no notice of our camp. I was blissfully unaware under my enveloping blanket. The next night I moved my bed away from my chosen tree to a place nearer the fire.

On one of our hunting days Christie thought he heard some elephants. He decided he would like to find them, just to take a look. He left me with the Land Rover and a loaded .22 rifle while he and his retainer went off on foot to find the elephants.

'If we are not back in an hour fire two shots in the air.' Fine, I thought, better than rattling about over rough terrain. I climbed on to the bonnet of the Land Rover and relaxed, enjoying the peace and quiet, listening to the ever present insect hum. I thought, not for the first time, about being cast adrift in this vast expanse of featureless bush; scrub trees scattered indiscriminately, sun browned grass, not much else; water in short supply, game widely dispersed and no evidence of a human population.

After a time of contemplation, comfortable in the shade of a tree, pondering the sheer vastness of the place and thinking gratefully of the predictable sun and the bisecting east to west track which saw us safely to our camp site each night it came to me that this was wild animal country. I moved inside and shut the doors. I hoped they would find their way back; I was beginning to feel lonely. After about forty-five minutes they appeared, much to my relief. They had not seen any elephants.

It was on the fifth day that Christie had a roan antelope in his sights. He held his position for a long time then lowered the rifle.

'In calf. I can't shoot it.'

This was a hunter playing by the rules. I was spared the killing. We left the next day empty handed. The day after I shaved off five days growth of beard, packed my bush soiled clothes and left for home.

I hoped Nkumba would prosper. It was out of my hands. For five days I had sampled the primitive heartland of Africa; for three years I had lived close to its people; I was destined never to return but I would take with me my memories.

This time it really was — *bye bye Tomasoni.*

Other titles published by
The House of Ulverscroft:

MANAGER BY APPOINTMENT

Ian Campbell Thomson

Sequel to *The Hired Lad.* This is the story of a farm and the people whose lives it touches . . . The 'hired lad' has been precipitated into farm management in the London stockbroker belt. The owner is 'big business', a city man, shunning country dress and pursuits but passionate about his land and his animals. The young manager had to adjust to handling diverse staff (including Land Girls), relate to wealthy neighbouring landowners and effect changes to the farming system. Two carefree friends enliven his social life, and romance is just around the corner.

MOGFORD'S WINNING WAYS

Ian Campbell Thomson

Life is proceeding peacefully on Mogford's farm and in the nearby village. The year is 1970 and spring has arrived. The cricket team is flexing its muscle. Blackie is making cider, guaranteed to enliven any gathering. Percy Percival has a new mare for the point-to-point. Will he gamble beyond his means? Mogford, with a sharp eye for a deal, is busy around the markets. Martha, his wife, does not always approve of his methods. Son Luke is not short of female admirers. Into this peaceful scene Betty Pringle arrives as a paying guest at the farm. And then there's the by-pass to split the village according to vested interests . . .